Through *My* Eyes

*Overcoming the Emotional
Injury of an Abusive Relationship*

Shari L. Howerton

© 2014 by Shari Howerton

All rights reserved under the Pan-American and International Copyright Conventions

Printed in the United States of America

This book may not be reproduced in whole or in part, in any form or by any means, electronic or mechanical, including photocopying, recording, or by any information storage and retrieval system now known or hereafter invented, without written permission from the author.

THE HOLY BIBLE, NEW INTERNATIONAL VERSION®, NIV® Copyright © 1973, 1978, 1984, 2011 by Biblica, Inc.™ Used by permission. All rights reserved worldwide.

ISBN 978-0-9888-9230-9
E-book ISBN 978-0-9888-9231-6

Cover design by Jennifer Yarbro
Mobile Artistry by Sheri Leseberg
Edited by Geoffrey Stone
Stonegate Publishing
geoffreydstone@gmail.com

www.ShariHowerton.com

To my husband and dearest friend,
John Howerton

You will always seem too good to be true.

Table of Contents

Foreword 5

Preface 7

Acknowledgments 13

Introduction 16

Chapter 1: How did I get into this mess? 22

Chapter 2: No Voice / No Boundaries 41

Chapter 3: Between a Rock and a Hard Place 55

Chapter 4: Self-Doubt 64

Chapter 5: A Frog in Hot Water 83

Chapter 6: The Holes in Our Hearts 97

Chapter 7: Conflict 113

Chapter 8: Fear 125

Chapter 9: You Are the Table 139

Chapter 10: Because He Can 150

Chapter 11: The Wedding / The Divorce 167

Chapter 12: Freedom 184

Chapter 13: Recovering 203

Chapter 14: Discovering Kindness 213

Chapter 15: Forgiveness 222

Chapter 16: Reflection 234

Epilogue 244

Suggested Reading 250

Foreword

My understanding of emotional abuse developed slowly over the years. I grew up next to some loud neighbors. The weekdays were quiet. The weekends were chaotic. The husband would often come home late at night intoxicated. His wife would have locked him out. My bedroom window faced their yard. I could hear the ruckus of beating on the door, begging, pleading, and threatening. Sometimes the police were called and that added to the drama. Often our neighbor spent a night in jail and his wife would bail him out the next day. That scenario played itself out for over a decade.

My mother tried to explain the dynamics to me. They were poor and had children, but the man was selfish and controlling. My mother understood that the lady felt emotionally dominated by her mate and that few options existed for her, but how do you explain "emotional domination" to a child? The drinking that was involved just intensified the action. Emotional abuse was devastating to our neighbor and her children. The pattern was never broken.

Shari has written a powerful book sharing her own personal nightmare of emotional abuse. Her life has been one of tragedy and triumph. In her first book Shari wrote about growing up in a cult-like church. The leaders were domineering and didn't respect the women in the church. When the people you look up to demean and belittle you, it crushes your self-esteem. Even with all of her personal strengths, she was "set up" to marry into an unhealthy situation.

Everyone's life is a tale of how their own self-esteem influences every area of their decision making. It is too easy to ask "Why don't you just leave?" Just as with my neighbors in my childhood, one has to understand the subjective world of the victim. My neighbor was not able emotionally to leave. As you read Shari's story, you will see how the forces had to work until eventually she felt more empowered.

I met Shari when she was a student at Lipscomb University. She was not your typical undergrad because of her maturity and life experiences. Yet her enthusiasm for learning and sparkling smile were captivating. She had just begun the "breaking away" process. She was trying to break the pattern from the past. Our sons went to the same private Christian schools so we shared a bond. Her faith in a good God was strong. I asked Shari to help as an observer in seminars for troubled marriages. People would come from across the country for a three-day intensive workshop to help rebuild their marriages. Because of her own experiences Shari had a natural empathy for the people at the workshop. Her insight into the pain and hope of others was remarkable.

In these pages you will read about how Shari was hurt and damaged by her husband, but you will also read about ultimate personal triumph as she gained strength that can come only from God as she sought Him in her life. God has blessed her with a new fulfilling life of power, and He can give you that freedom too if you will seek and submit to Him. The "take away" is that there is always hope for change and that the right decisions can break the cycle of past bondage.

Frank Scott, PhD LPC/MHSP,
Director, University Counseling Center at
Lipscomb University

PREFACE

"I rarely want an answer to a difficult question. What I want is somebody's story, and to find myself in their story. Answers feel lonely." — Donald Miller

I wasn't sure I would ever want to write this book. But I knew if I did, I would have to be convinced that my story could offer help, healing, and hope to others in similar circumstances. For several reasons I chose to completely avoid the subject of domestic abuse in my first book, *Breaking the Chains*, which is about my liberation from an oppressive religion. Even though the two aspects of my life are intricately intertwined, I chose not to write about my marital problems in that book because a brief chapter on the marital abuse that I lived daily for twenty-seven years wouldn't be enough space and I wanted to keep that book focused on spiritual abuse. It did not seem like the right time or place.

I was inspired to begin writing this book after reading a blog review of the book *Mending the Soul* by Steven R. Tracy. Just reading the review stirred memories and emotions within me. After reading the book review online (before the book even arrived) I wrote a blog post about my own abuse and shared Dr. Tracy's "Characteristics of Abusers." This prompted a fresh batch of urgings from friends to write my "other" book. So, I decided to try, though I was reluctant. I wasn't sure my stories would be helpful to anyone else, and I was hesitant to relive that part of my life. But as I began to write, the chapters flowed out of me. As I finished each chapter, I shared my writing with a handful of friends, and the feedback I got from readers of each new installment was encouraging: "Keep writing! You're going to help someone." I was convinced, and if this book helps even one person, my purpose is fulfilled in writing it.

As with any memoir, these are my memories and reflections. This book is written entirely from my perspective as an abused woman. Not even my son, who lived in the same house and experienced many of the same behaviors, can fully understand what it was like for me to live as a battered wife. While I have learned that there is no shame in being honest about your life's experiences, I still battle with being overly critical of myself and needing affirmation from other people. But aside from my own insecurities, I genuinely care about the feelings of others and don't like to hurt people with my honesty. Some may not understand why I have chosen to share all or any of these details. My motivation has not been self-therapy. Although, my writing has once again proven to be more liberating than I anticipated. And this book has broken a few more of my chains. I truly believe I have an opportunity to help others understand, manage, and even escape similar situations. I am so grateful to the authors of books and memoirs who have invited me into their painful pasts; they have helped me in my journey by sharing their experiences and struggles.

Likewise, after writing *Breaking the Chains* I received hundreds of messages from readers thanking me for my courage and affirming my perspective on the situation. A couple of people wrote that they resented my writing and thought my perspective was wrong. Many others felt strongly that I was "way too nice." That's why I specifically want to address the subject of perspective in this preface. While I have not lied, misrepresented facts, shaded or embellished the truth in either book, I have, of course, shared my own thoughts and perspectives on the events I have written about. And I make no apology for that. But I want to remind the reader that you are reading the author's perspective. And I don't mean to suggest mine is the only perspective.

Additionally, I want to make it clear that I am intentional about showing grace to those who have wronged and abused me in the past. Colossians 4:6 urges us to let our speech "always be with grace, as though seasoned with salt." It is my conviction that I will never regret being kind, though I do have one concern about my writing style; I do not ever want to be misunderstood as *minimizing* abuse, ungodly behavior, cruel words or actions. I simply believe that compassion for other broken people is important and healing. We are all broken, and I share *my* brokenness openly in this book. But God's grace is sufficient and His mercies are new every morning.

Sometimes writing about our collective brokenness upsets people. Not everyone wants to confront or be confronted in this way. After writing *Breaking the Chains* I found a couple quotes to be liberating as a writer:

> "When a book leaves your hands, it belongs to God. He may use it to save a few souls or to try a few others, but I think that for the writer to worry is to take over God's business." —Flannery O' Connor

> "Becoming a writer is about becoming conscious. When you're conscious and writing from a place of insight and simplicity and real caring about the truth, you have the ability to throw the lights on for your reader. He or she will recognize his or her life and truth in what you say, in the pictures you have painted, and this decreases the terrible sense of isolation that we have all had too much of."
> —Anne Lamott

As you read this book, keep in mind there are many manifestations of abusive behavior. My abuser was not abusive in every category. For instance, he never once attempted to exert power over me sexually, and he was not controlling with money the way many abusive men are. There may be ways I was abused that do not match your circumstances. And even though there are always worse cases out there, you should never dismiss abuse as insignificant on any level. The effects are always damaging.

In the book *Unbroken* by Laura Hillenbrand, she recounts the WWII experiences of Louis Zamperini. It is a moving and difficult story that includes the most heinous abuses inflicted on prisoners of war. Zamperini's abuse was beyond anything I could imagine. His experiences make my challenges look like a day at the park. And although I could not imagine the physical pain he endured, I identified with the emotional and psychological impact of the dehumanization. I was able to relate to the loss of personal dignity he experienced at the hands of mean, vicious bullies. I have never met a victim of abuse whom I could not relate to emotionally no matter how different our details.

In writing my story it was not my goal to recount every instance of abuse I could remember from twenty-seven years of marriage. Instead, I wanted to give you a window into what life was like for me living with a narcissistic man. More than that, I wanted to show that there is a way out, a window that leads to freedom. And that window is pried opened by what we believe. For so long *I believed* God required me to stay and be abused. Other writers, along with friends and counselors, helped throw the lights on for me to discover the truth.

Many authors who have written books on this subject differ in their view of the role enabling plays in abuse. In *Why*

Does He Do That? Lundy Bancroft states, "You are not 'enabling' your partner to mistreat you; he is entirely responsible for his own actions." But Gavin De Becker, in *The Gift of Fear*, says that we are only victims once; then we are volunteers (for abuse). Personally, I do believe I played an enabling role in my abuse. But I also agree that my abuser was responsible for his actions and I did not *cause* him to abuse me.

Confronting and owning my unhealthy behaviors *assisted* me in breaking free from an abusive relationship. I am transparent in sharing my mistakes in the hope that someone else may learn from them; *certainly not to over-emphasize my complicity in the abuse.*

As I wrote about my life between the ages of sixteen and forty-three, I was anxious to get to the end of my abusive marriage and tell the healing part of my history. I breathed an enormous sigh of relief when I began writing about the end of my marriage. The chapters that chronicle my marital abuse are difficult reading and were, at times, painful to write. But as you read, you will not have to wonder how the story ends or what became of me because I'm here to tell you that I have not only survived, I have thrived. And so can you.

What I want you to know before you read the very first chapter is that this is a story of restoration and triumph. My life today is good; better than I could have imagined. While writing about some of my darker days, I am occasionally tempted to give myself credit for being so resilient. But I know that God gets the glory. I often felt that I did not have what it took to overcome my circumstances within myself. But God was always there beside me, helping me through each and every situation I faced, just as I believe He will be right beside me for all the challenges in my future.

Whether or not you believe in God, I hope to inspire you to honestly examine the ways you may be responding inappropriately to abusive people. But I also hope to encourage you to look outside of yourself for strength. I don't like the saying that God never gives us more than we can handle. I believe just the opposite. I believe He gives us more than we can manage on our own so we will learn to depend on Him. And I hope that you will find strength in the cross of Jesus.

I am continually amazed by what God has done in my life. I remember a day when I begged Him to let me die in a car wreck because I didn't think I could possibly face what was ahead of me, and I couldn't take my own life. That was a long, long time ago, when there was no way for me to know just how God would use that very suffering to help others in the future. When I think about that day now, it brings both tears and a smile. I am reminded how God, knowing His plans for my future and how much I would want to live, lovingly did not answer that prayer.

I'm so thankful God does not answer all of my prayers according to my desires at the moment I'm praying.

Acknowledgments

To my son, Danny, thank you for encouraging me to share this part of my life. I thought about you constantly as I wrote this book, imagining myself in your shoes as a reader. And that was one of the hardest parts of my writing. I appreciate your willingness to embrace this exposure in the hope that my story might offer hope and encouragement to other victims of abuse. I love you and I am so proud of the man you have become.

To my husband, John, thank you for showing me such love and devotion. The love you have given me is the love I longed for the first forty-three years of my life. You were worth the wait. And the contrast between my past and my present makes me appreciate you all the more.

To my family members and former in-laws who choose to read this book, thank you for opening your heart to understand my heart and my journey a little better. I hope it will be apparent that I want to share these experiences for the benefit and healing of others in similar circumstances, not to hurt or embarrass anyone. I love and value every member of my family, past and present.

To Dad, thank you for not giving up on our relationship. In spite of some of the hard times we've been through, I have always loved you so much. I am thankful the prayers we have both prayed for healing and forgiveness have been answered.

I thank the friends who have shared their own stories of abuse with me. You know who you are. You have educated me. You have inspired me. You have enriched me. And you have always encouraged me to write on this topic. You have given my suffering purpose and meaning as I have been able to reach out and connect with you in genuine empathy primarily because I know what it feels like to be abused. Each of you has touched my life in a significant and powerful way. I cherish your friendship and trust.

I thank my editor Geoffrey Stone for agreeing to edit my second book. Geoff, your guidance and constructive criticism have made this book so much better. And through this process I have grown in my ability to depersonalize constructive criticism. Although few people who know me would believe that *I* would have to be encouraged to share more details, thank you for nudging me in places to add more. I dreaded the editing process with my first book, but looked forward to it with this one. It's been a privilege and a pleasure to work with you again.

Once again, I have been blessed with artistically gifted friends who have generously contributed their talent to provide me with a beautiful cover for my book. Sheri Leseberg and Jennifer Yarbro, I thank you so much for your time, talent and friendship. I thank my friend, Heather Lilly, for taking the original cover photographs. Those awkward moments on the beach provided good photos, as well as fun memories that will be tied forever to this book.

I thank my former professor and friend Dr. Frank Scott for writing the foreword. Frank, you are so wise, kind, and fatherly. You are easy to look up to even though you are only a *few* years older than I am. I value your friendship. And I have deeply appreciated your many words of encouragement. I want you to know that, as a cherished friend and mentor, it has meant a great deal to me each time you have said, "I am proud of you."

I thank Floyd D. Dawson, MS, LPC for the four years of Christian counseling that inspired me to confront my own toxicity. Floyd, your insight and encouragement played a critical role in my becoming the person I am today. I still reflect on and share many words of wisdom I learned from you.

I thank Dr. Steven R. Tracy for writing *Mending the Soul: Understanding and Healing Abuse*. It is the best book I have ever read on the subject. Dr. Tracy, your book helped me to better understand what the Bible truly says on this subject—and what it does not. *Mending the Soul* should be required reading for every pastor. But not just pastors. Every believer should be educated in how to be a compassionate friend, able to facilitate (rather than impede) the healing process of those who have suffered the damaging effects of abuse.

Last, but most important of all, I cannot fail to express the overwhelming thankfulness I have for my Savior; for His love, mercy, and grace; for dying in my place on the cross; and for His faithful provision throughout my life.

Introduction

"You can't grow without pain; you can't find your life's purpose if you aren't willing to embrace discomfort and join others in their suffering."
—Jeff Goins

This is a story about the pain and struggle of domestic abuse. It is also a story of self-discovery and lessons learned, both of which continue to this day. And it is ultimately a story of healing and restoration. In my journey it has helped me to read about the life experiences of others. Many of our most difficult experiences are isolating, so being reminded that I am not alone has always offered me both comfort and hope. That is why I want to pass along the details of my life's journey, to help you and me not only to accept suffering as a part of life but to embrace it as an opportunity to grow. There are things I regret in my life. My biggest regrets are the times I caused pain for others. But I don't regret that I have suffered.

In 2009, I wrote *Breaking the Chains: Overcoming the Spiritual Abuse of a False Gospel*. I was born and raised in a legalistic, cultish church in Southern California, where I grew up believing I was a Christian. We were taught that we had to attain literal perfection (equal to the sinless life of Jesus Christ) in order to receive eternal life. This "truth" was revealed to the founder of our movement, William Sowders, in the early part of the twentieth century and we, "the body," were called to restore the true church in the last days by sharing these special truths before Jesus returned. Needless to say, the doctrine of perfection robbed me of the grace that is found in the cross of Christ—that He died for our sin and that it is a gift unto eternal life.

I struggled with perfectionism at home as well. Our home was very structured. Some of my friends have shared with me as adults that although they loved my parents, the atmosphere of our home was so rigid that they often felt uncomfortable. My mom kept a spotless, "perfect" house. My dad was self-employed and worked from home, so he was always around. And both of them were strict disciplinarians. I was the oldest child, and I became an achiever, academically and musically. Like a lot of kids, I wanted to please my parents and make them proud. The way I did that was by excelling, earning straight As and performing flawlessly on the piano. I felt their displeasure most when I stepped out of line by asserting myself verbally. My mother said I was "mouthy."

Growing up my family would attend four church services a week with each one lasting two and a half to three hours. We did not miss a service unless someone was sick. Our lives revolved around our church and our pastor, Brother Mears, who we were taught to revere and obey as the man of God. He exercised a high degree of authority and control over our personal lives. He and some of our authority figures instilled fear in the young people when it came to disobeying or challenging Brother Mears' authority. To do so was considered rebellion and displeasing to God (like the Israelites' rebellion against Moses). Our pastor's rules were not always based on Scripture (other than the one that says to obey them that have the rule over you) but were based on his subjective preferences. He expected the women to wear their hair long and once forbid us to even trim our bangs until he said we could use scissors again. He was against makeup. Earrings were forbidden. He thought boots were masculine and should not be worn by women. He was opposed to backless (sling back) high heel shoes; he thought they were too provocative. He instructed the men to keep their hair short and not to wear facial hair. We were expected to check with him before planning a vacation or missing a service. We had to consult him before planning any social gathering in our homes. My son once started a Bible study for young people in our home and after three gatherings, he was told that he was trying to "usurp authority" and there were to be no Bible studies led by anyone other than the pastor.

In addition to Brother Mears having spiritual authority over *all* our lives, there was strong and consistent emphasis placed on men having God-given authority over women. One prominent pastor in our group had a saying: "Christ is the head of the man. The man is the head of the woman. And the woman is the head of nothing but the broom." Not every man in our church embraced this attitude, but when he would say this from the pulpit, Brother Mears would chuckle.

You can read more about my religious upbringing and my journey out of spiritual abuse in my book *Breaking the Chains*. I believe the spiritual abuse and oppressive attitude toward women during my childhood led me to fall victim to domestic abuse in the first place, and was the main reason I felt trapped in my abusive marriage for so long. I stayed primarily because I believed God expected me to endure the abuse and still be the best wife I could be in my circumstances. I was raised to conform, to please, to obey. People close to me consistently conveyed the message to me that my needs and emotions were an imposition, and my opinions were unwelcome. My parents complained that I was too emotional and too assertive. Growing up, they seemed to believe that I contributed to any and all mistreatment I experienced. Their response when I had any kind of relational problem was always, "Well, what did *you* do to cause [such and such]?" I was not encouraged to stand up for myself. And while I'm sure they believed they were being balanced, not wanting to think their child was never at fault, it felt to me like my parents never went to bat for me.

One big example stands out vividly in my memory. I was bullied at school my entire seventh grade year. I was physically, as well as verbally, assaulted. My dad's advice was to turn the other cheek. When I told him that *teenage girls I had never even met* were coming up to me as I waited for the bus and punching me in the arm, claiming I called them a whore, he told me to let them hit me. He explained that it wouldn't be any fun to keep hitting someone who wouldn't fight back, and they'd eventually just go away. Yet I remember when my younger brother reported to my dad that he was being harassed on the school bus by some of the other boys, my dad told *him* to punch back. Even though the bullying I endured was (in my mind) so much worse, my dad reacted differently to his boy being intimidated. My brother could make Dad proud by standing up for himself. I could make Dad proud by letting girls hit me until it wasn't fun anymore. And this was after I had already been nearly dragged into a bathroom during lunch one day where a gang of girls intended to beat me up behind a closed door. I managed to cling to a pole until they gave up. I begged two boys from my church who were standing nearby to knock on the door of the teacher's lounge (a few steps away) and get my counselor to help me.

When the bullying did not stop, my parents met with my school counselor. He told my parents that he had interviewed some of these girls himself, and they said they didn't like the way I looked. My parents thought they were jealous, but I did not feel pretty. I felt like a weirdo because I was not allowed to dress like everyone else (our church had a strict dress code that required girls to wear long skirts). I never fully understood why they bullied me, but I just wanted my parents to protect me.

Obviously I survived that rough year, but I've always looked back on seventh grade and wondered why my parents didn't stand up for me or pull me out of school. They could have sent me to a private school. The experience is long behind me. I don't hold this against my parents. But as a parent myself all these years later, I still can't say that I understand why they did not do more to defend and protect me. If you think I felt less important to my dad because I was a girl, you would be right. I don't think my dad would agree that he valued me less, but I remember how awful that year was for me and how I felt inside. In hindsight I suspect the messages my parents sent to me about my worth played into my willingness to accept marital abuse for twenty-seven years. I believe they loved me and tried to do their best, but I also believe they diminished my sense of self worth.

My ex-husband was raised in the same church group, but with a completely different family dynamic. His parents divorced when he was in high school, and his mother leaned heavily on him to take on the role of the man of the house, to be the surrogate dad to his little sister. She also instilled a lot of fear in him that he would struggle with throughout his entire life. She constantly told him to never let anybody hurt him; especially in regards to the girls he dated. As a result, his having the upper hand in every relationship was extremely important to him. I'm fairly certain his need to dominate and have the upper hand was a big part of his attraction to me. There was a power imbalance from day one. And certain patterns in our relationship were established early.

Dennis and I met when he was twenty-two and I was fifteen. However, I believe it was my personality and not just my age that Dennis gravitated toward. I have always been a pursuer with an open, transparent heart. I crave affirming words and emotional reassurance that everything is okay in all my relationships. I am a communicator and am extremely expressive. If someone withdraws from me, I feel compelled to reach out and pursue communication. I love to nurture people; make them feel special. I believe most of these personality traits to be inborn, but my environment certainly played a role in my development. I wasn't aware of it at the time but now I realize that Dennis used these traits against me to manipulate me. When he was in a bad mood and would give me the silent treatment, without even knowing it I did the worst thing I could possibly do. I pursued him and tried to coax him back into harmony, reconciliation, communication, a good mood. I tried to prove myself and prove my love—over and over for twenty-seven years. I jumped through his emotional hoops until I had depleted every reservoir. I fought for the marriage and its potential all the while not realizing that I was giving him exactly what *he* was craving—power and control.

In a healthy relationship couples share responsibility; they willingly own their part in conflict. In a relationship with a narcissist, it is never his (or her) fault. It is always something the other person did and he (or she) will always try to manipulate the other person into believing they were wrong. That is what Dennis did to me for twenty-seven years, and I played right into his game.

In these pages you will see how Dennis manipulated me and how I fed his narcissism by coddling him. Your experiences may be different, but I hope that my story will shed some light on any unhealthy dynamic in your relationship. And I hope that my happy ending may be an encouragement to you.

Chapter 1
HOW DID I GET INTO THIS MESS?

"Why does a twenty-two-year-old man pursue a sixteen-year-old adolescent? Because he is stimulated and challenged by her? Obviously not. They are at completely different developmental points in life with a dramatic imbalance in their levels of knowledge and experience. He is attracted to power and seeks a partner who will look up to him with awe and allow him to lead her." —Lundy Bancroft

IT WAS OCTOBER 29, 1975, A WEDNESDAY AFTERNOON. It was exactly one week to the day after the newlyweds had eloped. The bride was sixteen years old. The groom turned twenty-three just two days after the ceremony.

They had married in the Santa Barbara Courtyard with only the groom's family present. The groom's older brother and his wife had generously given them the wedding gift of a honeymoon in San Francisco. And they were now home, settling into their small rented apartment.

A discussion turned into a disagreement and the groom began to lecture the young bride who was eating an ice cream bar at the kitchen table. It was unacceptable for her to disagree with him and he was becoming increasingly agitated. Sitting across from him at the kitchen table, she kept looking at her ice cream instead of making eye contact with him as he spoke condescendingly to her. Suddenly he stood up and shoved the ice cream in her face, rubbing it on her cheek and down her neck. "Oh, you *like* that ice cream, huh? How do you like it now?" he said mockingly. She didn't like it one bit and told him what she thought about it. The arguing quickly escalated and she hurried to the bathroom to escape his wrath. Before she could close the door, her new husband pushed his way in, grabbed her, and held her against the wall. His size was intimidating. He was six feet four inches and weighed well over three hundred pounds. She was five feet four inches and 132 pounds.

With his left hand he held her against the wall as he drew his right fist back and stopped short of hitting her. She was terrified, believing she was about to be punched in the face. She had seen him get angry before, but she had not seen that kind of rage. He had never been physically violent, but then again she had only dated him for six months.

After she cowered in fear and told him how sorry she was for ignoring him, he let her go. Within minutes he began to apologize profusely. Surely she knew he would never actually hurt her. Would she forgive him? Yes. Of course, she forgave him. And that was the beginning of a cycle of abuse that would last for twenty-seven long years.

This young girl's father had urged her to "just run off and get married." He informed his daughter that he wouldn't be attending her wedding no matter where or when it was anyway. She was a disappointment to him. And he was angry with her. He told her she was a cheat and a liar. And he didn't care if she ever set foot in his house again. "Just go," he insisted.

He was upset because of a truancy notice that came in the mail. The notice stated that she had missed her high school PE class on more than one occasion. It was the only class she had following the lunch period. When confronted by her father the young girl had explained that she had gone to an off-campus lunch with her fiancé and had decided not to go back to school for PE. She had never really liked PE and didn't consider it an important class. What was the big deal?

She had felt a lot more grown up than she actually was following her recent engagement. She didn't understand why her dad was making such a mountain out of a molehill. Backed up by her fiancé, she offered a weak apology. If she had known her father would get so irate and go on a tirade, she would have tried to feign deeper regret. But instead, she became defensive, which only intensified her father's anger. He seemed astounded that his daughter could take ditching school so lightly. He lectured her on the importance of honesty and integrity and tried to make her see that this behavior was the beginning of her "moral fibers decaying." Up to this point, she had always taken school seriously. And he was alarmed by the recent change in her attitude.

It was true. She had always been an academic achiever and a rule follower. For most of her life as a student, she had gotten As and Bs, but mostly As. She sang in her junior high chorus and in the smaller group of Madrigals in the ninth grade. She had been a concert pianist as a youngster, practicing daily. She had even received special permission from the school board superintendent to graduate midterm her junior year. And she would be graduating with honors. She had definitely taken school seriously prior to her engagement.

Her boyfriend had not. He thought her father was too strict and did not hesitate to say so. He did have a point. She was weeks away from becoming a wife, yet she still had a bedtime and a curfew. Her fiancé enjoyed making wisecracks about such ironies. He reveled in sarcasm and resented authority. He had shared with her that, although he had the talent, he did not play football in high school because *no coach was going to yell at him*. He had recently dropped out of college due to bouts of depression. And it was shortly after that when the two had met.

When this young girl was about to turn sixteen her future husband made his appearance in the church where she had attended all her life. He played tennis a few times with her dad. And she was flattered when he began to show an interest in her. After several conversations before and after services, he asked if he could take her out on her first date, and she happily accepted the invitation. Within a few months, he proposed.

Her new boyfriend could be charming and persuasive. But he could also be confrontational. And he was quickly replacing her father as the primary male influence in her life. Her father believed it was his corrupting influence that had convinced his daughter to view skipping school so casually.

Although he had formally given his permission (she could not have legally married without it), this soon-to-be bride's father did so primarily because he was convinced she would do something rash and impulsive if he didn't. The thought of his daughter having premarital sex or running away in rebellion must have seemed worse to him than getting married too young, and so he gave in. He was not only suffering from a broken heart, but a loss of control. So when he blew up at her for skipping school, he was no doubt transferring a lot of pent up frustration. It had to have been hard to see his little girl marrying the first guy she dated. Although he was no doubt carried away by his emotions, the cruel words were wrong just the same.

The outburst had been a shock to her. First he yelled a lot and then he lectured her on her moral fiber. Then a little time had gone by. She thought he might cool off and have a change of heart. Instead he had called her into his room, asked her to sit down, and then proceeded to tell her in a calm, collected tone that he had no interest in attending her wedding and she should just elope. He had already signed the paperwork giving his legal consent, so she was free to go any time she chose. It was at this point that he said he was so disappointed in her that he really didn't care if she ever set foot in his house again.

She didn't say much during that conversation. But walking down the hall from his room to hers, she cried as she took it all in. It seemed surreal that her father could be ready to disown her simply because she had skipped a PE class or two. She was devastated. She was confused. She wondered if she could have kept the situation from escalating by responding differently. But it was too late for that. She wondered if her mother felt the same way her dad did.

Her mother had retreated into privacy and cried. Even if she disagreed with her husband, she was not the kind of wife who would ever fail to present "a united front," as her mom always said. She did not challenge him openly, although she may have done so privately (to no avail). Later in the evening, after the young girl had secluded herself in her room and started to pack, her mother knocked on the door. She wanted to give her daughter a gold bracelet she had bought for her in Hawaii as a wedding gift. And she wanted to tell her that she loved her. It was evident that her mother had been crying. Obviously her father had not spoken for both of them. She desperately wanted to ask her mother, "Don't you think Dad was wrong to say such hurtful things to me?" But she saw the pain in her mother's face and didn't want to make it worse for her. She was thankful for those loving, affirming moments.

What now? She wanted to get married. She had actually dreamed of a formal wedding all her life. But her fiancé had talked her out of it. He did not want a wedding. He didn't want to have to wear a tux and found the whole formality of the event unappealing. He asked her if she really wanted him to be "standing up there sweating, uncomfortable, not enjoying a single minute of the ceremony." Wouldn't she rather forego all of that if it made the wedding more pleasant *for him*? He seemed to make a good argument for the discomfort ruining the meaning of the ceremony.

He was persuasive, but also she was not strong or confident enough to tell him how much a wedding meant to her and that her mom would be deeply disappointed if her only daughter chose not to go through with the formal wedding plans. No, she already knew that expressing either of those as reasons for going through with a formal wedding would elicit a lengthy lecture intended to inflict guilt for putting anything or anyone ahead of her groom and what made him happy. After all, he should come first; before her mom and before her own desires. That was the way she had been taught marriage should be. And her mother was the perfect role model.

Her fiancé had already overruled many aspects of the wedding that she cherished. She had asked her childhood friend to be her maid of honor as soon as she was engaged. When she started discussing her bridal party with her fiancé, he was emphatic about not including the friend because of something ridiculous. It was a huge red flag that she missed because of her desire to please. She was already trying desperately to keep the peace by compromising her own desires.

The increasing stress of her fiancé's demands and preferences was taking the fun out of planning the wedding. His heart clearly wasn't in it. He kept lobbying for a private, family ceremony followed by a reception that everyone could attend. It seemed like his biggest issue with the wedding was that he would have to wear a tux or a suit. He was so focused on his own comfort above all else. Eventually, they agreed to forego the wedding.

The bride's parents had bought a trunk full of cans of mixed nuts and dinner mints. A deposit had been paid for her dress. Bridesmaids' dresses had been selected. As she was an only daughter the bride's mother was emotionally invested in the traditional ceremony and celebration. Not having a ceremony was going to break her mother's heart, and she wasn't looking forward to making this announcement. Then the truancy notice came, followed by her dad's reaction. Even though it was bad timing, they went ahead and told her parents that they had recently decided they didn't want the formal wedding. The announcement likely contributed to her dad's extremely harsh words. After all, it wasn't as if she had been a wild child or caused her parents a lot of anguish as a teen. She had actually been a pretty good girl, trying to make her parents proud through her achievements.

She turned to her fiancé for comfort and reassurance that she wasn't such a bad daughter. And after a lengthy conversation, they decided to drive up the coast to Santa Barbara the next day and get married.

One week later, she experienced a display of rage like none she had ever witnessed, including the threat of physical violence. But she convinced herself to take that rage in stride just as she had tried to take in stride her father's anger. And this decision set the stage for many years of abuse to follow.

§

That young girl was me. I say "was me" because the young bride depicted in the first part of this chapter is someone very different from who I am today. I remember her. I hurt for her. I feel sorry for her. And yet I also feel angry and frustrated with her. She enabled her abuser from the very first week of her marriage.

The fiancé was my husband Dennis. I say "was" because he passed away in 2011. I wish I could tell you that he changed and became a better person over time. He did not. He was narcissistic and abusive right up until the day he died. Today I would never subject myself to that kind of abuse. And I'm thankful I got out when I did. I was spared the downward spiral of his last nine years.

Of course, in retrospect, through the clear lens of healing, I believe I had an active role in facilitating my abuse for nearly three full decades. It would be so easy to look back and judge my sixteen-year-old ignorant self and want to shake "her." But I can't sit in judgment of her. Everything I know today is the result of all those years. While she had no tools, no resources, no education, and only the life experiences of her sixteen sheltered years to work with, I have the knowledge of what finally liberated me to make different, healthier choices. I know "the rest of the story." And I hope that my story will help someone else not to have to endure the same experiences.

What's hardest about owning these experiences is not the embarrassment to me but the embarrassment to others. The first week of my married life is incomplete without the puzzle pieces of why I eloped and why I felt I could not turn to my parents for support following that first incident of domestic violence. So the complete story needs to be shared. But I don't enjoy sharing the details because they reflect poorly on my father. I don't want readers to judge my dad. I don't want to minimize the wrong and hurtful behavior, but my heart feels compassion for my dad's inadequacies as a father. My dad suffered abuse as a child. I'm not excusing him because of that.

I just recognize the wounds of abuse and neglect. Therefore, it has always been easy for me to forgive him.

My parents might have tried to help me if they had known I was in a violent situation. But they didn't know because I protected my abuser and his reputation at my own expense. I can only speculate that they might have tried to help me because of the reality that later on, when they *did* know, they seemed to feel helpless to do anything. Perhaps, because I was so protective of my abuser, they didn't think there was much they could do. And I don't fault them for that.

I sometimes think that enablers are born, not made. I believe I was born with certain personality traits that contributed to a propensity towards enabling. But there are certainly elements of my upbringing that contributed to my being an enabler and thus an ideal candidate for an abusive relationship. Unquestioning submission to authority was insisted upon from my earliest memories. And men were to be obeyed simply because they were men. This played out at home in my dad's strict parenting style. One of his philosophies on raising children was that you had to break a child's strong will early. When I was young I remember my dad frequently saying that I was a strong willed child whose will needed to be broken. At a very young age, I would hold my breath when I got mad, and my dad's method for making me catch my breath was to turn the water on in the bathtub and stick my head under the running water. He laughed when he told the story and said that snapped me right out of it and forced me to breathe. We now live in a different day and time. Today that would be construed by some as abuse. Back then it was perhaps more acceptable to do things like that to control your children. I'm quite certain my dad didn't think he was doing anything harmful to me.

I don't think my will was ever completely broken. Instead I think my dad affectively weakened my ability to stand up for myself by whittling away at my spirit. I think today more parents realize that the goal should be to break a strong will so that the child learns to obey but not break her spirit so she becomes submissive and susceptible to abuse. A strong will can certainly be an asset in facing life's challenges as an adult, but a broken spirit will almost always lead to despair.

One of the ironies to my being a victim is that I can be pretty assertive in some situations. Outside of my marriage I was anything but a doormat. But with my husband I certainly was. My role as enabler evolved out of fear and self-preservation, wanting to be loved. But most of all I wanted to be a good wife. And I was taught that being a good wife meant not speaking up for yourself. I have very few memories of my mom challenging my dad (in front of us) on anything. My understanding of what was desirable or acceptable in a wife, and certainly what was pleasing to God, was formed at an early age. And that led me to accept being dominated by my husband as normal. At the time, I didn't truly know how abusive my circumstances were. My outlook on life was that everybody had their problems. And I had mine.

※

After I wrote *Breaking the Chains*, I learned something interesting my mom once said to my kindergarten teacher during a parent teacher conference. My former teacher told me that reading my book had brought to mind this conversation, which she had previously forgotten. She asked if I remembered my boyfriend in kindergarten. I did, of course. His name was

Brett. I also remembered that we told our teacher we were going to marry each other when we grew up. (I remember thinking I would marry every boy I ever liked.) She thought it was cute and shared this with my mom, expecting my mom to think it was cute as well. But my mom became quite serious and informed her, "Oh, no. Shari will marry in the church."

My former teacher, Ms. Kirschner, told me that she was taken aback and didn't know quite what to say to my mother. She wanted to laugh and say, "We're talking about five-year-olds." But she didn't. She told me she thought highly of all the parents in our church, whose kids she had in her classes. We were all quite well behaved and good students. She didn't know much about our beliefs or restrictions at the time. But she did think my mom's response was a bit odd.

I never knew about my mom's comments until forty-five years later. It kind of surprised me that my mom would be that transparent about the church rules. (By the time I left the church, these kinds of "rules" were being denied.) I guess I wasn't aware of those restrictions at age five, but long before I was dating age I knew I had to date within the church. And I knew I was allowed to marry with my parents' consent at the age of sixteen only because I was marrying within our church.

୨ଡ଼

All of my vivid memories from those first years of marriage are bad memories. It wasn't that there were no good days, but they are eclipsed by the dark depression and the flashes of rage that could appear without warning. I was also abandoned on a fairly regular basis. Episodes of rage or depression would flare up at even the smallest offense. A minor disagreement quickly would turn into a full blown war, and my husband would say he wanted a divorce and then walk out. Sometimes he'd be gone for hours and other times days. Sometimes I'd be left without transportation. Sometimes he'd tell *me* to leave. There were many separations.

One time I came home from the grocery store to find him sitting on the floor in the corner of a spare bedroom looking depressed. I asked him if he was okay and he said, "I'm sorry. It's not you. It's me. But I have been thinking about this, and I am just not cut out to be married. Would you call your parents and ask them if you can move home?" I can still visualize him sitting there, looking up at me, wearing those baggy denim overalls he would wear day in and day out.

Believe it or not, I promptly did what he asked. My parents were perplexed. I know they must have thought it was bizarre. *It was bizarre.* But what could they say? They of course took me in. And in a few days he was calling and begging me to come home because he missed me. He said he didn't know what in the world he had been thinking. And I went home and picked up where we left off as though it hadn't happened. I actually felt grateful.

Another time he told me that he needed to lose weight (he was one hundred pounds overweight at this time) and get healthy, but he couldn't do it without making major changes in his life. He decided that in order to get healthy he needed completely different surroundings. So he was going to leave me and go live with his brother in Santa Barbara for a while to get healthy. End of subject. It didn't really matter how I felt about his decision or how it would affect me. It was always all about him and what he needed. So he drove the 130 miles from our home in Chino and temporarily moved in with his brother and sister-in-law. I can't remember how long he stayed. It might have been a week or two, but he quickly figured out that it wasn't his address that needed to change.

The erratic behavior began immediately in our marriage. It happened before our son was born and, I'm sad to say, it continued on all through Danny's high school and college years. My husband said that I was the cause of his anger, and when he got mad he would just leave. In the early years, he'd most frequently go to his mother's to cool off. She had treated me as if I was her rival from the get go, and I could only surmise that she was sympathizing with him, validating his behavior. Sometimes he would go visit his brother. I didn't know what he was saying to them on these visits. I just assumed I was being blamed for our problems. If only they could have seen the mess he usually left in his wake.

I'll never forget the day my mother dropped by unannounced and did see it. Dennis had just blown up. He had thrown against the wall every piece of glass he could lay his hands on (even picking up wedding gifts from our coffee table). Then he walked out, leaving me with a small baby and shattered glass everywhere. When he would explode and destroy things, he would always leave the mess for me to clean up alone. I cannot remember one single time he cleaned up his own mess. That was my job. My mom had never seen the evidence of his temper before. She was appalled. She asked if I wanted her to help me clean up, but I told her it would be a bigger help if she just took Danny for a while. Thankfully, he was in his crib when the explosion occurred.

By the third decade of our marriage we were living in Tennessee and Dennis was still buying and selling real estate in California. Although it was feast or famine regarding cash flow—there were times we experienced financial stress waiting for deals to close—Dennis was successful and took pride in his ability to wheel and deal. He earned a good living and we were able to travel back and forth. So at that point, when he would blow up, he would hit the road for California in the blink of an eye. That's how he dealt with problems. He took off. He ran away. By that time I was relieved to see him go. Even though I knew it was just a brief break in the action, I learned to enjoy those vacations from dealing with his outbursts, his moods, and his constant emotional demands.

Dennis was like a Jekyll and Hyde. On a good day, in the right circumstances, he was a great guy and people liked him. He had a quick wit. He cracked people up, including me. He could be charming and fun to be around. He could be genuinely warm, personable, and caring. But almost everyone he was in a relationship with on more than a superficial level eventually saw his dark side. If he felt slighted, if he didn't get his way, if his demands were not met, he lashed out in anger. There were many fallings-out with business associates and friends because of Dennis' explosive temper. There would be periods of time when he wasn't on speaking terms with certain friends or business associates and then times when he was back on good terms with them. It went in cycles. He had a favorite escrow officer who was also a close friend. When their relationship was friendly, she was like family and he even stayed with her and her husband on a few of his trips to California. But when he got mad at her, he would tell her off and hang up on her. (She also hung up on him). And they wouldn't speak for months. But then they would repair their relationship and go on. It wasn't as if he were only unreasonable and difficult at home. He could be a monster in any relationship given the right circumstances. But he was the most abusive to me.

I can't even remember the number of times he abandoned me when he was angry. It was a routine part of my life. I just learned to accept it as a way of life. It's amazing what you can take in stride when you are an enabler. One night, though, stands out from all the rest. It was Christmas of 1978, our son, Danny's, first Christmas. Dennis got mad and blew just before Christmas. We fought all the time, so I can't even remember what the fight was about. But it was especially predictable around the holidays. Well, this Christmas, Danny's first Christmas, he left us.

I took my baby to my parents' house and spent Christmas Eve there. Danny was the beloved first grandson and my parents did the best they could to make it a merry Christmas. But I have a rather pitiful picture of myself from that Christmas Eve with an expression of deep sorrow and hopelessness. To this day seeing that picture triggers a wave of sadness. I remember feeling so alone. I was not only hurt and disappointed that my husband would miss our baby's first Christmas in order to display his petty anger, I was also extremely embarrassed.

Even the so-called good days were unstable because the smallest trigger could turn my world upside down in a flash. There was almost constant fighting; especially in the earlier years. And even when we were getting along, I was treated like a slave. It was my job to serve him.

One of the things you cannot do with a narcissist is say no. If you deny a narcissist, the consequences are extreme, disproportionate to the situation. During these early years, it was not unusual at all for my husband to strike me with an open hand, push me against a wall or knock me down on the ground. He would throw objects and slam doors so hard pictures fell off the walls.

I lived my life trying to avoid unwanted consequences. I am convinced that Dennis suffered from full blown narcissistic personality disorder. I also believe he was bi-polar. And he even had symptoms of borderline personality disorder. But there is no question in my mind about the narcissism. And when a narcissist asks you to do *anything* for them, it's not simply a request. It's an expectation. A narcissist feels entitled to whatever they want. You are also expected to figure out what they want or need even when they don't tell you specifically. And when (not if) you fail to meet their demands, their wants, their perceived needs, you become their enemy. You are immediately vilified. And anything could be turned into an offense. It could be something of minor consequence. It could be something completely unintentional. It could be my choice of words or the expression on my face. It could just be the mood he woke up in that day. Life was precarious even on the good days because I knew everything could change in an instant.

During the earliest years of our marriage I was a naïve, trusting teenager trying to get along with a troubled and complicated man who mistreated me almost daily. I perceived my biggest problem as being emotional and expressive. I reacted. I was unguarded. I had not learned how to filter my reactions or choose my battles. And I *needed* to please him in order to be validated by him. Needing to please was my part in the toxicity.

It's hard to remember specific details of how our fights started because we fought about everything and nothing. He didn't go off on me because I burned his toast or didn't have dinner on the table at a certain time. He was not demanding in those ways. He was emotionally demanding. I could never figure out how to satisfy him or anticipate what he needed from me. I guess only another woman who has lived with this kind of man will completely understand what I'm describing when I tell you that he had such a deep hole inside him, it could not be filled up. I realized many years later that he loathed himself and transferred that to me. But I was far from being able to comprehend the psychological dynamic I was living in at that young age. I was in way over my head.

It was like I was continually on trial to prove my loyalty to him. He expected me to cater to the whims of his mother and sister, but he constantly criticized my family and expected me to side with him against them. If I disagreed with his perception of anything or anyone, he couldn't handle it. He had to prove that he was right and I was wrong. And if I didn't agree with him, I was disloyal to him. I remember praying and asking God why we had to live in constant turmoil. *Why couldn't we just have a normal argument like other couples and not have it escalate into hellish proportions?* To say that Dennis made mountains out of molehills would be a grandiose understatement. He blew everything out of proportion and became enraged over the smallest things. Every time he got mad, he blamed and belittled me. He frequently said our marriage was never going to work; we should just give up and get divorced. He said I provoked him and brought out the worst in him. He even made fun of my appearance and made hurtful comments about my weight after pregnancy yet he was one hundred pounds overweight. He would become irate if I ever mentioned his weight, but he could say anything he wanted to about mine.

We had a huge fight one time when we were in Santa Barbara to visit my in-laws. This was in our first year of marriage. He wanted to go hit some balls on the racquetball court, and I put on a pair of shorts and a T-shirt to join him. Because of our strict church dress code, I didn't wear shorts out in public. But I thought they were appropriate for the racquetball court. Dennis didn't approve of the way I looked. He humiliated me, telling me how bad I looked in shorts. It seemed clear to me that this was not only about our church rules; he was embarrassed for me to wear them on his former college campus. I thought he was afraid he would see someone he knew. I had gained about ten pounds since our wedding at this point. He was far heavier than I was, but if I had ever insinuated I was embarrassed to be seen with him, there would have been major fallout. There was always a double standard with him and I was deeply hurt by his reaction. We wound up screaming at each other so loudly, the next day the neighbors asked my sister-in-law jokingly if everything was okay.

We fought any time I didn't immediately comply with his requests. And we fought any time I asked something of Dennis that he didn't want to do. That's how he taught me not to ask him to do things. And I'm talking about little things like taking out the trash or hanging up his clothes. In all the years I was married to him, he never hung up his clothes. Not only did I have to walk on eggshells to avoid setting Dennis off, I had to comply with all of his unreasonable demands, and I had to appear to do so willingly. If I complied unwillingly, that would still result in a verbal assault. He routinely asked me to go out late at night to get fast food for him. When asked to go out for Taco Bell and snacks from the local 7/11, I knew I couldn't say no without unpleasant consequences. Even when it was 11:30 at night and I told him I was afraid to be out that late by myself, he didn't care. It would escalate into a full blown fight, and often he would give me the silent treatment for days if I refused to do his bidding. I rarely felt brave enough to refuse him. The price I would pay for ever saying no to him was high. I tried to accommodate him most of the time to avoid his explosive anger, but I was often unsuccessful.

I will never forget the time my late night food runs came up in conversation with my mom. I was not even eighteen years old. Naturally, she was shocked that I was being sent out regularly so late at night and was concerned for my safety. My mom had a little "trademark" grin at times when she was trying to make her point in a nice way. She would raise an eyebrow and smile, as if to say, "Really?" or "You expect me to believe that?" She looked at Dennis with that little grin of hers and said, "I suppose if something terrible happens to her, you'll just tell me you're sorry?" He laughed it off but later remarked to me privately that it was none of her business if I went out alone at night and he certainly wouldn't owe her an apology if something happened to me. The contempt for my mom's concern was blatant. How dare she suggest he would be responsible if something happened to me? He took responsibility for nothing.

Chapter 2
NO VOICE / NO BOUNDARIES

"There will be inevitable violations of boundaries. More than vanity, arrogance, self-absorption, or any of the other traits we commonly think of as narcissistic, this is your biggest clue to another person's narcissism. Ignore it at your own risk." —Sandy Hotchkiss

IN MARCH 2011 MEREDITH BAXTER WAS BEING interviewed by Oprah Winfrey on television about her memoir *Untied*. Even though many years had passed since I had left my ex-husband, her words resonated deeply within me, giving me goose bumps. Oprah brought up an example of physical abuse Baxter had shared in her book, but then confirmed that ". . . the relationship was not as physically abusive as it was emotionally and verbally abusive, would you say?"

Meredith responded, "Right. And the truth is, you don't have to be abused physically too many times . . . a couple of times, and you know that's always on the back burner. That can always come. It's the continuing corrosive effect of being belittled, denigrated. . . . I had no voice for so long."

In that moment I was flooded with memories and overwhelmed with emotion. I sat glued to the TV. As Baxter spoke her voice broke, and I could see tears in her eyes. Here was someone most people would describe as a powerful, successful woman. And she knew precisely how powerless and helpless I had felt. I knew instinctively that she had experienced the same abuse, that her words were genuine. You never forget what it feels like to be treated that way. No matter how many years pass or how much you heal, you never forget.

There was more emotional and verbal abuse than physical abuse in my marriage too. I never had injuries that required medical attention. The physical violence was a method for conveying who had the power and control, and he demonstrated that early in our relationship. He had anger issues and very little self-control. I don't think it was always calculated, but I do believe he enjoyed putting a little fear in me from time to time. He was a bully. He wanted me to know who was in charge, just in case I ever doubted it, and I never lost sight of what he was capable of. When he pushed me and I fell to the floor, he laughed at me mockingly in flagrant contempt. It was demoralizing. The belittling was worse than any physical pain ever inflicted.

Dennis mocked and belittled me out of his own insecurity. He was so emotionally needy he did not want me to feel confident or self-reliant. If I did, he was afraid I might not need him, so my personal growth was a threat to him. The insults, put-downs, and sarcasm were his way of keeping me feeling insecure. If he was in control of how I felt about myself, he could manipulate me to serve his agenda. Early in the marriage, while I was in my teens and twenties, I didn't have the maturity or the wisdom to understand these dynamics. I was intimidated. I was afraid. I believed he had all the power and I had none. I was so filled with self-doubt that I often sincerely agreed with him that I was to blame for our problems. He was an expert at verbal sparring, and I was no match for him in those early years. He frequently told me that my family didn't love or respect me, and he tried to alienate me from independent women friends. Through all of these tactics, he was able to keep me constantly off-balance, insecure, fearful, and at his mercy.

By doing this he could foster a sense of self-worth in me when it suited him, and he could jerk the rug out from under me any time he felt like it.

Dennis tried to intimidate me into complete silence. He effectively invalidated anything I tried to say to the point that I felt I had absolutely no voice in anything. His constant calculated mind games perpetuated my continual self-doubt. Although I didn't give up on my attempts to communicate from my heart until the very end, for all my attempts at honest communication I *never* felt as if my voice was truly heard except when he felt in eminent danger of losing me permanently. And then he would become attentive and open to self-examination just long enough to win me back. He would make desperate promises in those moments; promises that were never kept but always gave me hope of real change, and held me emotionally captive.

The effort to silence my voice was evident in every aspect of our relationship. I was completely dominated by Dennis. He didn't have any respect for me, and I didn't know how to go about effectively establishing, maintaining or enforcing personal boundaries. I had never been taught how to stand up for myself. Compliance was the virtue everyone seemed to want from me. And in my marriage to Dennis, I was required to do his bidding and serve as amusement, even when his humor was at my expense.

One afternoon in 1982 I was in the kitchen preparing a big dinner of turkey and homemade dressing. I was washing out a dish at the sink while celery and onions were sautéing on the stove. On a whim, Dennis walked up behind me and put his hands around my throat, cutting off my oxygen. I couldn't talk and he didn't seem to get the message from my body language that I couldn't breathe. He squeezed my neck and laughed while I struggled to convey my distress with arm movements. It was a very scary experience. Not being able to breathe, I remember my thoughts: *I'm going to die and he's laughing.* I lost consciousness and went completely limp in his hands. As he lay me down on the floor, my arm hit the handle of the sauté pan. Hot butter splattered and burned my legs. When I came to, I was convulsing from lack of oxygen, my legs were burning from the hot butter, and he was in my face yelling at me. I was disoriented and my first thought upon regaining consciousness was not to question *him*, but to question *myself*. *Why is he yelling at me? What did I do wrong?* I thought. This is how an abused person thinks. *I* must have done something to *cause* what is happening to me.

Once I fully regained consciousness and the disorientation passed, Dennis explained later that he was just having a little fun. He stressed repeatedly that he had been joking around and thought it would be funny to pretend like he was choking me. But when I passed out he got scared. Although this happened during a stressful period of time, when it was widely known among friends and family that we were having serious problems in our marriage, we were not fighting that day, and he had not intended to hurt me. He said his greatest fear was that nobody would believe he'd only been playing if he had killed me. He was frantic as I was lying there on the floor. However, even when he thought I might be dying, his thoughts were of himself. He wasn't afraid that he might have really harmed or killed me! He was afraid that he would be held responsible if he did! To this day (more than ten years out of the marriage), when someone is frustrated around me, often my response is, "What'd I do?" It's my autopilot.

The experience frightened me, but I laughed it off. It almost seemed like a blessing in disguise because the rest of the evening he went overboard in kindness. Kindness was not something I enjoyed regularly and it was so comforting. He kept asking if I believed that he had not meant to hurt me. He apologized over and over, and I assured him the entire night that I believed him and it was no big deal. This became a funny story that was occasionally told to friends. But looking back, knowing everything I know today, I don't find it amusing. What kind of man walks up behind an unsuspecting woman and squeezes her throat for a laugh? It was a sadistic way to have fun, but I never thought about it that way at the time. I was desensitized to the aggression because it had become such a familiar aspect of my young life. I believe to this day that he had not intended to harm me. He really did think it was funny. Even his humor revealed a dark side.

Numerous friends have told me in recent years how they hated the way Dennis always made me the butt of his jokes. The laughs were always at my expense. They told me that I never acted like it bothered me. That I would just laugh right along with him. I explain to them that the constant put-downs did bother me, but the jokes were the least of his abusive behavior. Those jokes were nothing compared with the way I was often treated in private. And when I tried to express my hurt feelings, my voice fell on deaf ears.

Objecting got me nowhere. Dennis rejected anything construed as criticism. Anything that even hinted at inadequacy in him provoked a hostile response. Much later I read that these traits were defined as textbook narcissism. It was such a relief when I finally started to see, in black and white, that a true narcissist's behavior makes the victim feel crazy and overwhelmed with self-doubt. That was exactly what I was living. If I tried to express my feelings about something specific Dennis had said or done, he would blow up. He would turn the tables on me, saying how he could never please me or say sarcastically: "You have such a terrible life, don't you? Was it rough going out to lunch with your friends today?" He'd go on a tangent about how I didn't appreciate him, and he was only as good as the last thing he'd done for me. He would twist my words into something I was not even saying (disloyalty and a lack of respect or appreciation) so that I would wind up apologizing and explaining myself. He even boasted to me once that he had many times successfully convinced me I was wrong when he knew I was right, so I should never expect to win an argument with him. He laughed with amusement at my expense when he informed me of that. Communication was not relational with him; it was one of the ways he mentally toyed with me.

Sometimes the conversation would deteriorate into my defending or apologizing for a word choice, my tone of voice, or the expression on my face. I was not a perfect wife, but I was constantly trying to figure out how to make things better. Because a better marriage was truly my goal, I tried to look within myself for the areas where I was the problem. Once, in the middle of a serious conversation, he interrupted me and told me to go into the bathroom and look at my expression in the mirror so I would understand why he was upset and defensive. I actually complied, returned to the conversation, and agreed with him. I then tried to explain that I'm expressive and don't intentionally make a face that will be offensive.

These tactics were his way of winning through intimidation. He put me on the defensive and manipulated me into responding to his accusations so he wouldn't have to listen to anything I was trying to say. And if he didn't go on the attack, he would simply belittle me for being too sensitive. Repeatedly I resorted to writing letters to him just so that I could express myself without interruptions, insults, and manipulations. He rarely apologized. Sometimes I would find the letters or notes discarded in the trash. Sometimes he would respond angrily. Every once in a while, he would respond by acting normal again or cracking a joke as if nothing had happened. But how we proceeded was always his option to exercise. I was like his little puppy dog, waiting for a pat on the head and willing to do anything for my master. Puppies don't talk. The most they can do is bark or whimper when mistreated. Looking back, I realize that my voice was no more than barking or whimpering to Dennis; noise to be silenced.

When Meredith Baxter shared with obvious emotion that she had not had a voice for so long, I knew exactly what she was talking about. I suddenly and unexpectedly relived the despair of my own oppression as if I had escaped only a day earlier instead of years earlier.

The physical abuse I suffered was the most frequent in the first seven years of our marriage, when I was in my teens and early twenties. I was pregnant with my son at the age of eighteen. And there were episodes of mild violence during my pregnancy. Mildly violent seems like an oxymoron. I know. But that is how I thought of it. After all, I was not being beaten up and sent to the hospital. Instead Dennis would *only* shove me hard enough to make me lose my balance and fall, slap me with an open hand, or grab me in a threatening way. It was more about frightening me than injuring me. He once hit me repeatedly with a shoe, and another time he kicked me in the side while I was on the floor (after pushing me), but it wasn't hard enough to injure me. That is one of the ways I now know he wasn't necessarily physical because he was out of control, since he was able to restrain himself enough that he didn't ever inflict serious injury or pain that would require medical attention. But at the time, I believed his anger caused him to lose control. Occasionally, he would compare himself favorably to actual wife-beaters and remind me that he wasn't kicking the crap out of me like some men, as if to suggest I was lucky he didn't.

During my pregnancy it wasn't the physical abuse I worried about. I believed Dennis would always stop short of putting the baby in jeopardy. Instead I worried that my unborn child would suffer physically from the emotional stress and strain I was under throughout my pregnancy. I was being verbally battered and emotionally abused regularly. I cried a lot and experienced what I now know were anxiety attacks. Back then, I would have described it as my nerves being bad. One night as I cried on the couch after a fight, I prayed that my child would be unaffected.

While six months pregnant, Dennis and I got into an argument about finances. He had been on unemployment for a while and was sensitive about it. I said something that he perceived as an insult. He thought I was calling him lazy. I tried desperately to explain that whatever I said, I had not intended to imply any such thing. But he went ballistic. He went to the store and bought some beer. He didn't normally consume alcohol, so I knew his drinking was for dramatic effect. It was his way of getting back at me for saying something he didn't like. He didn't just have a few beers. He drank beer after beer, from the numerous six-packs he brought home from the store. I sat on the bed in the next room and heard the pop of every can he opened. I wasn't counting them, but they were many. I was actually pretty traumatized by this. I had never been around anyone who drank alcohol and had never seen Dennis drink before. He belched loudly as he became intoxicated. It was disgusting. I was scared, and I didn't know what to do. I certainly couldn't call my parents and let them know what was happening. That would be too embarrassing. And they would never forget. So I called his mom. She came and got me. And I spent the night at her house.

Dennis ultimately wound up there too. But I stayed away from him, in another room. His mom tried to sober him up by spoon-feeding him chicken soup. He had made several drunken statements about how he intended to start living his life from now on. "The beer's gonna flow!" he bellowed at one point.

The next day, after he was sober I found out that at some point that night, he had a friend take him to a local 7/11 to buy more beer where he called an old college girlfriend from a pay phone and tried to arrange a date with her. He had brought her to church with him just before we started dating. She was beautiful, and he reminisced about her a lot. I had been intimidated by her beauty and felt inferior to her. She was not available to meet him right then, but they made a date for later in the week (which he wound up canceling). He asked my forgiveness, and, of course, I instantly forgave his destructive behavior. From then on that night became a joke within his immediate family. Everybody laughed about it, including me.

Our son was born a few months later. And I was so relieved when Danny's pediatrician commented on what an exceptionally calm newborn he was.

There was more yelling, throwing, slapping, and pushing after Danny's birth. I had mistakenly believed that Dennis would stop short of physical intimidation as long as I was holding the baby. I was wrong. Dennis pushed me onto the bed once while I was holding Danny in my arms. I was standing in a small space between the bed and dresser of a very small bedroom. The push was not enough to hurt me. But it certainly could have hurt Danny if he'd hit his head on the dresser or fallen from my arms as I lost my balance. I was shocked that Dennis would risk that. But he was irrational when he was angry.

When Danny was still a toddler, Dennis announced out of the blue that our marriage probably wasn't going to last and he didn't want to risk bringing another child into the world with me, so he was going to have a vasectomy. I told him I wasn't willing to be sterilized, but it was fine with me if he wanted to. He had me find a surgeon and schedule an appointment. (He never made his own appointments for anything).

I always thought his reasoning was bizarre. Since he was still in his twenties it seemed to me like he might want to have a child with someone else if he didn't expect our marriage to last, but I didn't question him. And not having another child with him was fine with me. As I look back, though, I can see that Dennis' vasectomy was yet another way for him to be in control. It was his way of telling me that having another child *with me* would be so terrible that he was willing to forfeit ever having another child with anyone. I got the message, and it was okay with me. I had always imagined having two children, but I didn't feel like I *needed* to have another. I also knew it wouldn't have mattered if I did want more. I didn't have a say in the most inconsequential decisions, so I certainly knew I didn't have a voice in this significant decision. By this point in the marriage, I felt irrelevant and powerless.

Boundaries within relationships ideally secure comfort, safety, privacy, identity and order. They define where one person ends and another begins. Personal boundaries are like property lines we ask others not to cross, respecting the limits we set on behavior and communication we consider unacceptable both physically and emotionally. It's our responsibility to set these limits and enforce them. However, an abusive person rarely respects the boundaries of others. When our boundaries are violated, there will be frustration, anxiety and stress. I routinely experienced this stress, but I could not have defined it for you this way. These are things I learned much later.

I have learned that there *should* be a "me," a "you," and an "us" within relationships in order to balance closeness and separateness. When one person dominates a relationship, there is always a lack of regard for the boundaries of the party being dominated. People can violate someone's boundaries through the use of sarcasm; by turning or walking away and refusing to listen; by mocking, hitting, and throwing things; by lecturing, threatening, or acting condescendingly; by pushing buttons, being demanding or rude, refusing to take "no" for an answer, blaming, manipulating, or excessive teasing; the list is extensive and these are just a few examples. I experienced all of these violations on a regular basis. Dennis used all of these tactics to keep me in a state of fear and powerlessness. I cooperated with him more often than I challenged him. I was trying to be "a good wife" according to the teachings and examples of my youth. I didn't know what healthy boundaries were within a relationship or that it was my responsibility to set these limits and enforce them, *even as a Christian wife.*

I would not describe myself as a compliant child. In fact, I have memories of my maternal grandmother calling me "Contrary Shari." But I do remember frequently observing the *rewards* of compliance. In my family and in my spiritual environment, compliance was a desired and valued trait (especially in women). I wrongly believed I would be more *lovable* if I were more compliant. I now realize that my belief in compliance as a virtue influenced my role as willing counterpart to a narcissist.

Why is it Always About You? by Sandy Hotchkiss is one of the first books I read that defined for me not only Dennis' narcissism, but also the ways in which my social history and feelings about myself influenced my responses to him.

I longed for my mother's approval and her affirmation that I was acceptable as I was, but I often felt that I had to be something I wasn't in order to live up to her expectations. I actually have many of her traits—traits I've become aware of more and more as I have gotten older—but we are/were very different women temperamentally. I'm more transparent with my emotions and my mother was good at not revealing too much. She was good at putting on a "respectable" front despite whatever she might have been feeling inside. I remember well an incident that highlights our differences and my inner conflict.

During one of many separations from Dennis, I was sitting in church one Sunday next to my mom. What made this separation different and far more painful for my mom was that I had done something wrong that brought embarrassment to my family. Those details will come further into the book. But let it suffice to say that I was pretty certain my mom felt humiliated by me and for me. What I felt was deep remorse, conviction, guilt—and of course shame. But my shame had little if anything to do with pride. I just felt like a horrible person—in God's eyes, in people's eyes, and in my own eyes.

I was overwhelmed with sadness for having hurt people I loved. I wasn't feeling sorry for myself. At that point, I felt responsible for everyone's pain and believed I deserved contempt along with whatever punishment or suffering God required. I was so broken that there were tears rolling down my cheeks. My mom thought I was drawing attention to myself.

My mom had a close friend she greatly admired. Emma was very proper and in control at all times publicly, like my mom. Regardless of whatever she went through privately, this friend had a smile on her face and her chin was up. You would never know from her countenance that she was hurting. Her tears were not on display for others to see. And this was the kind of daughter my mom would have been most proud of in that moment, had I been able to comply with her protocol. Unfortunately (for my mom), I was anything but that person. I produce more tears the harder I try not to cry.

In that awkward moment, my mother leaned over to me and whispered, "Why can't you be a good little actress like Emma?" In my mind, this was just one more confirmation that I wasn't a daughter my mom could be proud of. I didn't think I was someone that anyone could be proud of. If only I *could* have complied, I *would* have; just to be the daughter my mother wanted.

My mother was my role model as a woman and as a wife. She was proper, private, reserved, and submissive to my father in front of her children. If she spoke up for herself, it wasn't in my presence. She deferred to him even when he was wrong. And this is what I was taught was pleasing to God in a wife. On the contrary, I am by nature feisty, assertive, and emotional. But I remember feeling, as I was growing up and as a young adult, that those were unattractive traits I needed to suppress in order to be acceptable and liked. I experienced a good deal of inner conflict between being who I was and who my mother was. I remember wanting to be like her and not wanting to be like her at the same time. I wanted to be myself, but I also desperately wanted to be a *good* daughter, *good* sister, *good* wife and mother. I lacked the words of affirmation that I craved and mistakenly bought into the belief that my inborn *personality* kept me from being a *good* anything. And then I transferred my affirmation seeking from my family to a narcissistic man who enjoyed manipulating and controlling me.

In *Why is it Always About You?* Sandy Hotchkiss explains that the first step in dealing with a narcissist is to know *yourself*. "Our social history from the very beginning teaches us what to expect from others and how we are to feel about ourselves. That is why our number-one tool for dealing with the Narcissist is to examine our own experiences and recognize how our reactions contribute to our discomfort. The goal is to understand what is happening and interrupt the process to protect ourselves."

As I began to examine my experiences, relationships and social history, along with my discomfort and my reactions to Dennis, I realized that I was conditioned to accept not having a voice or healthy boundaries before I even met Dennis and long before I knew what healthy boundaries were.

Chapter 3
BETWEEN A ROCK AND A HARD PLACE

"The abusive man's high entitlement leads him to have unfair and unreasonable expectations, so that the relationship revolves around his demands. His attitude is: 'You owe me.'" —Lundy Bancroft

AN ABUSIVE MAN DOESN'T MAKE A LOT OF PROMISES. When he does promise something, it's to get what he wants. And he doesn't keep those promises. An abusive man lacks empathy for others and does not give himself emotionally to his partner or to the relationship. Dennis expected to be catered to, deferred to, and agreed with even when his demands conflicted with my needs and values; even when I had to override my personal desires or convictions to satisfy his demands. If I chose not to do what he demanded, he would insult me and degrade me with cruel words, followed by days or weeks of silence. At the worst, this is a form of emotional terrorism. At best, it is bullying. The hardest part for me was that his sense of entitlement prevented him from ever recognizing the impact his behavior had on me. Whenever I tried to tell him how his behavior made me feel, he would respond sarcastically, describing how *good* I had it. The real problem, in his view, was that I didn't appreciate him or respect him as I should.

If I tried to have a conversation with him about my feelings, he twisted my words, causing me to defend myself instead of addressing a specific issue. No matter how gently I spoke or how carefully I tried to choose my words, whenever I attempted to tell him something that bothered me, his response would be, "I just don't do anything right. Do I? Nothing makes you happy. It sounds like you have a miserable life." I wasn't ever saying that, but I always wound up defending myself. If I disagreed with his opinion about a member of my family, he turned that into a loyalty issue and accused me of siding with them against him. If I confronted him about a joke he made that embarrassed me or asked him not to undermine me as a parent by making light of me in front of Danny, instead of responding to the issue at hand, he would always find a way to put me on the defensive and change the subject. He refused to hear the smallest criticism, reacting as if I had waged a full scale attack on him as a man. And any request was perceived as an unwelcome imposition.

An abusive man also manipulates situations to his advantage. One way Dennis did that in our marriage was that he would become irate at any request I would make of him. One evening we were getting ready to have dinner with my brother, Chris, and sister-in-law, Cheryl. Dennis enjoyed Chris and Cheryl, and we were both looking forward to a fun evening. I walked into the guest bathroom after Dennis had walked out and found a hot match laying on the marble countertop beside the sink. He always lit matches instead of using air freshener, and he would lay the match on the sink instead of throwing it away. Normally I would have thrown it away without saying anything to him. Whenever I asked him to try to do something different around the house, he would get defensive. He would overreact and say that I was nagging him, deliberately making it painful for me to ever ask anything of him. But at the time we were in the process of building our "dream home," and I didn't want Dennis burning a brand new countertop, so I spoke up. Being very careful with my tone of voice, I meekly and gingerly asked, "Dennis, could I ask a *favor*? Would you *mind* not setting hot matches on the sink in our new house? I'm so afraid one of those matches will cause a burn mark."

You would have thought I had accused him of murder. In an instant, he went from calm and pleasant to hostile and irate, shooting back, "I earn the money to pay for that house, and I'll put matches on the sink any damn time I want! Don't tell me what to do! Do you hear me? I'm getting sick and tired of your complaints. We don't even have a real marriage anymore. We are just two people living in the same house. This marriage isn't going to survive." That was a typical reaction to my asking a small favor of him. A reasonable request on my part was twisted into an assault on Dennis' freedom, his role as the breadwinner, and evidence that we didn't have an actual marriage.

We continued to argue on the drive over to Chris and Cheryl's. He kept insisting that we didn't have a marriage and I didn't appreciate him. I went into my usual posture of defender of the marriage, assuring him I did appreciate him, and I unsuccessfully tried to convince him that his reaction was out of proportion to what I had asked. I pleaded with him to please let it go and not be angry. But to no avail. I was surprised he didn't just drop me off and leave. That would have been more typical in one of these situations. Instead, he went into my brother's house and sat down in the living room with Chris while I went straight into the kitchen. I was close to tears and whispered what had happened to Cheryl. She knew Dennis' temper and how I lived. She just shook her head and said, "I'm so sorry." Dennis didn't speak to me again that evening, and he didn't stay long. He announced he was going home and left; Cheryl offered to give me a ride home when I was ready to go if I wanted to stay a while longer. Of course I did. The last thing I wanted to do was go home with Dennis. All this drama was my punishment for asking if he would *mind* not putting hot matches on a sink. As if I needed to be reminded that I had no right to ask anything of him.

Narcissists perceive requests as demands and you don't get to make demands of them; they make demands of you. They have such a sense of entitlement that you will either find a way to meet their demands or you will suffer consequences. It's as simple as that. Of abusive men, Lundy Bancroft writes, "For each ounce he gives, he wants a pound in return. He wants his partner to devote herself fully to catering to him, even if it means that her own needs—or her children's—get neglected. You can pour all your energy into keeping your partner content, but if he has this mind-set, he'll never be satisfied for long. And he will keep feeling that *you* are controlling *him*, because he doesn't believe that you should set any limits on his conduct or insist that he meet his responsibilities."

ॐ

Just after we were married in 1975, Dennis convinced me to drop out of high school. He appealed to my desire to be an adult and questioned why as a married woman I would want to spend my days on a high school campus. He suggested that I could finish up by going to adult school later on. In hindsight, it's unbelievable to me that I let him persuade me to drop out when I had only two months until my graduation, especially after I had worked hard to graduate early. I even received special permission from the school board superintendent to graduate midterm my junior year, which was not only a great accomplishment, it was a privilege. But from my earliest memory of our relationship, I felt like I had to go along with what he wanted or suffer unpleasant consequences. There were *always* unpleasant consequences for opposing him, so I tried not to. And not only did I want to avoid his wrath, I genuinely wanted to make him happy. I believed that was what a good wife was supposed to do. What I realize now is that my desire to please and his desire to control were a disastrous combination. Even though he was the one who had convinced me to quit school, I endured *years* of high school dropout jokes, followed by *years* of GED jokes after I finally went to adult school and passed the GED exam.

No matter how hard I tried to do what he wanted, I always felt like I failed. No matter what I did I would suffer. I now know the term for the predicament I was in all those years. In psychology, it's called a "double bind," *a choice of equally unfavorable options*. It was this way with my employment. When I worked Dennis would want me to stay home. When I stayed home, he would berate me and say that I wasn't contributing anything. Neither option was favorable.

Most of the years we were together, Dennis was self-employed. When I married him, he painted houses and worked at a steel company for a short time, which was the only time he ever punched a clock. Other than that, he stuck to a career path that offered the freedom to set his own hours. When Danny was a baby, Dennis suggested we get our real estate licenses and work as a team selling houses. Going into real estate appealed to me because of the flexible hours, but also because I didn't need a high school diploma.

Dennis thrived on being the breadwinner and receiving praise. I knew what success meant to his ego, so it was completely acceptable to me for all of our real estate sales to be recorded in his name. Even though we worked as a team, the commission checks and the prize points for contests were always credited to him. Any plaques or awards were made out to him.

He felt entitled to receive all the glory since he was the man and the breadwinner.

When he was doing well financially, he'd say he didn't want me to have a job. He didn't want me working outside the home because I wouldn't be able to take off whenever he wanted to go out of town or do something on the spur of the moment. Eventually, he got into real estate investing, buying neglected properties and rehabbing them to sell for a profit. He also worked as a loan officer and an account executive at different lending institutions. For the most part he made a good living, and we didn't need extra income.

When he was making good money, he enjoyed being the breadwinner and was content for me to stay home or work part time. But when we fought, he would hurl insults at me, saying I didn't contribute anything financially. He said I was dead weight. Before (and a few times after) I got my real estate license, at Dennis' suggestion I took clerical positions at local businesses to help out financially (a weekly paycheck as opposed to straight commission sales). Early in our marriage, I was only sixteen or seventeen, so I had to lie about my age. Those jobs were brief. Dennis wanted the additional income, but he preferred my dependence and availability to him. After a few months, Dennis would want me to quit, and I was happy to oblige. Once I had Danny, I wanted to be at home with him, and I wasn't raised to have career aspirations. I didn't have a lot of confidence in myself, nor did I have a drive to "be something," other than a wife and a mom.

I never loved selling real estate. I did it because Dennis wanted me to, and it provided flexibility with our schedules. In the best of times, we made a good team, and we were successful. But living with *and* working with an abusive man definitely presented its challenges. We could not work together harmoniously any time there was unresolved conflict, which was often. And there was an imbalance of power in all aspects of our relationship, including business. He was the one in charge, and I was expected to do whatever he disliked doing. It was more like I worked *for* him instead of *with* him. In spite of that, there were times when we worked well together. There were times I even enjoyed the reward of being a successful team. However, daily life with a person like this is emotionally draining. Our life followed the cycle of abuse like a merry-go-round: tensions building, incidents happening, reconciling (the honeymoon phase), and periods of calm followed by new tensions building. In our twenty-seven-year relationship, we never did successfully break out of that cycle as a couple until I finally left.

In the late eighties I took a part-time position at Pomona Valley Escrow, working as an escrow officer assistant for a friend and business associate, Jan. My general office skills and real estate knowledge made me a good candidate for this position. My job was to open escrows, order title information, and produce the escrow instructions for the real estate agents involved. The actual escrow officer would handle it from there.

I loved that job more than anything I had done previously. The work environment was fast-paced and sometimes stressful, but it was often fun. I was well liked. I took pride in my work. I received a lot of praise from my boss, Jan. She paid me well, and I was such a valued employee that Jan was always trying to persuade me to go full time. It was rewarding and felt good to be valued by an employer and friend, but the happier I was there, the more Dennis seemed to dislike my working. The dislike turned into resentment, and he began to put pressure on me to quit. He did not like Jan's business partner, who was also my boss, and he would say, "If *you* have to answer to Margie, *I* have to answer to Margie. And I'm not going to answer to Margie every time I want to take off and go somewhere. You need to tell them you're done."

My boss never gave me a hard time about taking time off, as long as I gave them a little advance notice. The real issue was that I loved my job, and I was getting a lot of recognition for being smart and capable (independently of Dennis). He wanted to be the only one who could make me feel a sense of worth or worthlessness. He didn't want me to have a sense of accomplishment apart from him. He feared I would gain confidence that could lead to a feeling of independence. It was just so ridiculous that he wanted me to quit after years of berating me for not having any drive or fulfilling my potential. He wanted me to earn income, but he was obviously threatened by my personal growth and achievement.

Just as this same man who convinced me to drop out of school often made fun of me for being a dropout, he swung back and forth between claiming he didn't want or need me to work to belittling me for having no drive or aspirations. One of his favorite put-downs when he was mad was to call me "dead weight." He derived great satisfaction in giving me "a life of leisure" (his words), and then took equal pleasure in using it as a weapon in nearly every argument, frequently claiming, "I am nothing but a meal ticket to you!" And then I would go into overdrive assuring him that was not true. My escrow job took that weapon out of his hands, and because it was the one job I truly enjoyed, it was hard for me to give that one up. I kept making the argument that I was earning a paycheck and enjoying what I was doing. I reminded him of how many times he'd complained about my not having any drive, not contributing financially. He relentlessly pressured me to quit, so finally I told him I would quit if he promised he would never say I was dead weight again. He did promise not to insult me that way anymore, but it turned out to be another empty promise just to get his way.

Over the years I held a few more jobs, some full-time and some part-time, but Dennis would always eventually want me to quit. My marriage and Dennis' happiness were both important to me. With the exception of Pomona Valley Escrow, I never *loved* working outside the home, so it wasn't like he had to strong-arm me. I was always *willing* to quit. The frustrating thing was not that he *forced* me to quit jobs, but rather that I could never please him no matter what I did.

Chapter 4
SELF-DOUBT

"He did not love you if he exploited your vulnerability. If he really loved you, he would have been your friend." —John Howerton

PERPETUAL EMOTIONAL ABUSE RESULTS IN EXTREME vulnerability and a fragile sense of self. Even ten years after the end of my abusive marriage I still at times feel fragile and vulnerable. I once struggled with crippling self-doubt. The self-doubt I experience today is far less incapacitating.

Although there are times when I stand strong in my convictions, I have moments of anxiety to this day when I second-guess myself. My self-scrutiny sometimes takes on a life of its own, consuming my thoughts. One of my biggest fears has always been anyone viewing me as a bad person or as having a bad motive. My anxiety has frequently been triggered by criticism, especially criticism coming from someone I deeply love and value. Even when I believed I had done the right thing with the right motive, I might be quickly enveloped in a dark cloud of self-doubt. It's not simply that I would question my decision or motive. My self-doubt would occasionally leave me questioning *me*; what kind of person I am. I have hated those fragile moments. Although I recognize *why* I have had this struggle, even that knowledge hasn't completely enabled me to break free of it. But I have made great strides in this area even in the last year.

My abuser knew I was plagued with this self-doubt, and he used it to his advantage by attacking my character and motives.

Dennis would tell me how I *really* felt and insisted I was lying if I said he was wrong. "That's not how you really feel . . . that's not what you meant . . . that's not why you said it . . . you *intended* to hurt me" he would assert. I felt that my heart was always questioned. I would defend myself by saying, "I am not a bad person." When I would sink into the self-doubt and verbalize what I was feeling, he would laugh and say, "I never called you a bad person. *You* must think of yourself as a bad person since you always need to prove that you're not."

For so many years I was conditioned to feel responsible for the bad things that happened that I became a chronic apologizer. I even apologized frequently for the way I felt. Long after my divorce, I remember a conversation with Danny in which I was telling him about apologizing for something I hadn't even said. I had been falsely accused by someone of something and was tearfully accepting responsibility for their interpretation when my son interrupted and reminded me, "Mom, you are apologizing for something you didn't even do."

That's how I lived my life for so many years. The smallest conflict would set Dennis off. He would assassinate my character, question my motives, and strategically twist my words. So I developed a habit of trying to anticipate every possible scenario and direction the conversation could take. I thought that if I could figure out how to choose the perfect words, I could avoid any unwanted consequences. But it is impossible to avoid consequences when dealing with an abuser. They constantly need someone else to blame. A person with an open heart and a desire to accept responsibility for their role in conflict is the easiest to manipulate emotionally. The abuser uses their victim's sincerity and desire for resolution against them because the abuser's goal is not genuine resolution and relationship but rather power and control. (This is one of the reasons it can be so dangerous for well-meaning Christians—who do not understand the mind of an abusive man—to give advice to an emotionally/verbally/physically battered woman!)

I remember a friend, who did see my relationship clearly, once telling me, "Shari, Dennis uses you against you." In *Mending the Soul*, Steven R. Tracy explains it this way: "Abusers are often very cunning, and they deceitfully prey on the very virtues of those they abuse, counting on the fact that their victims will not act treacherously, as they do."

Aside from, or perhaps hand-in-hand with, the fact that I was sincere and had a desire to take responsibility; I was also conditioned spiritually to doubt myself. I addressed the damaging effects of spiritual abuse in my first book, *Breaking the Chains*. I believe that my severely legalistic upbringing not only causes me to battle perfectionist tendencies to this day, but it also contributed to my past acceptance of domestic abuse. Throughout the entire twenty-seven years that I subjected myself to abuse, I believed I was doing what God expected of me. I was young and believed that God wanted us together no matter what. My pastor continually reinforced that idea, which is why I stayed with him so long, and even remarried him after a brief divorce in my twenties. It wasn't until I was forty-three that I finally broke the chains of that marriage for good.

༶

Throughout the early years of our marriage, Dennis frequently reminded me of how lucky I was to be with him. I don't remember him ever saying that he was lucky to be with me. I never felt special to him. I never felt like he appreciated or valued me. I didn't feel loved. I felt taken for granted and abused.

Dennis frequently battled depression. He exhibited major mood swings. His temper was unpredictable. And he was severely overweight. At times he was antisocial. He was only comfortable with a few close friends and often refused to accompany me to any event where he would have to dress up. I went to church by myself most of the time. I went to weddings alone. I often had to go by myself to social gatherings, even Christmas programs that our son was participating in as a little boy at church. If I dared even to ask if he was *thinking about going* with me, he would get angry and snap at me with this familiar phrase: "Don't hassle me!" He almost always got depressed around Christmastime. He dreaded all major holidays and routinely picked fights to avoid having to participate in family gatherings. I was never sure if it was conscious or subconscious, but it was predictable.

In late 1980, Dennis was extremely overweight. He didn't even know how overweight he was. He had refused to step onto scales (even in the doctor's office) for so long that he had no idea what he weighed. He decided to go on the Optifast liquid diet and had to be weighed at the beginning. I remember his shock and horror at the initial weigh-in. He was at his heaviest, weighing 427 pounds. He was six feet four inches tall and large boned, but there is no such thing as carrying that amount of weight well. He followed the plan faithfully and started rapidly dropping pounds. He got very thin. He ended up losing more than one hundred fifty pounds. His lowest weight was around 240, but because of his frame, he looked like he was less than two hundred pounds. He had never looked or felt better and he became a happier person, but I became even more insecure. I was fearful of what his weight loss would mean for our marriage. I thought that if he believed I was lucky to have him when he was at his worst, he would surely feel even more superior to me after he lost a lot of weight. I figured he would think that he could do better, and it was only a matter of time before I would be dumped. After all, this man had routinely abandoned me so many times before. My self-esteem was near zero. I was in a dangerous place mentally and emotionally, but I didn't recognize it.

At this same time, I was helping a friend try to sell her house. Her friend George (not his real name) was helping her do some repairs. And one day when I had an appointment to show the house, George was there working. George was my longest childhood crush. I never dated him, but we were raised in the same church, and I was infatuated with him from the time I was about six years old and he was ten or eleven. Going to church four times a week provided plenty of opportunities to see each other and flirt, even though I was too young to date. I ditched school twice in seventh grade to spend the day with him (for which I got in big trouble when my parents found out), but all we did was hang out and talk, nothing more. I had always thought he would be my first date when I turned sixteen. I actually thought I might marry him one day (I always thought about boys in terms of marriage—perhaps because of my religious upbringing), but we both ended up marrying other people.

George's wife was thin and pretty. I knew her. We were not close friends, but we had grown up together in the church, and I loved her whole family. She was the reason I didn't date George when I turned sixteen. He didn't wait for me to turn sixteen. It hurt my feelings at the time, but I got over it. Because I had gained weight after marriage I was self-conscious. I was racked with insecurity and felt unattractive. I was also nervous to be at the house alone with him while I waited on clients who never showed up. Trying to make casual conversation, I innocently said something that led to disastrous events. "I bet every time you look at me you're glad you didn't wind up with me," I said with a laugh. He did not laugh. His expression turned serious, and he said, "Shari, I have never once looked at you and thought that." He later added, "Actually, I have always loved you and wished I could have married you. I think you're beautiful."

He told me how special I was and shared his regret over having made decisions that messed up our chances of dating when I turned sixteen. It felt warm and cozy, like curling up in a soft blanket. Nobody had ever made me feel special; certainly not my husband. It was not about physical attraction. Getting involved with a man other than my husband had never even been a passing thought, but I was emotionally aroused. I felt a rush of conflicting emotion in those moments. I knew the conversation itself was wrong, but it smothered my self-doubt by building me up. Nothing happened that day other than conversation, and that ended abruptly because I felt uncomfortable and left. Then the phone calls began. George started calling me and pursuing me emotionally. He kept telling me how he had loved me since we were kids and had never gotten over me. He just wanted to talk to me. We weren't doing anything *that* wrong, I tried to convince myself. He complimented me and made me feel desirable. I still remember how seductive his words were and how weak my defenses were. It wasn't about being told I was pretty or sexy. I just wanted to be loved, wanted, and needed by someone. I wanted to feel important to someone, and he made me feel like I was a prize. Dennis not only neglected me and took me for granted; he never wanted to build me or my confidence up in this way. He wanted me to view *him* as the prize catch and be afraid that he might leave me permanently one day.

The growing emotional attachment to George was wrong, and I felt terribly guilty. But I didn't want the kind, validating words to end, and after all, I justified to myself, all we were doing was talking. It was like a barrier came down then. I enjoyed George's attention. It was like rain falling on desert sand, and I soaked it up. I enjoyed feeling special and desirable to someone. I have never used drugs, but I've been told that some narcotics are so addicting you cannot try them once without being hooked. Kindness and affirmation were those drugs for me. I started looking forward to the calls and even feeling like I needed them to get through the day.

Shortly after we began talking on the phone, George started showing up at the gym when he knew I was there working out. I would be walking on the track, and he'd just appear beside me. We'd walk together and talk about our lives. He and his wife had lost a baby, and he shared how hard it had been on him. Everyone rallied to his wife and her emotions, he told me, but nobody seemed to recognize how difficult the experience was for him. I shared with him that I had been abused physically and emotionally. He reacted in anger as though he wanted to protect me. One day when we were alone on the track, he stopped, looked at me, took my face in his hands, then gently and tenderly kissed me. Another barrier came down, and I remember thinking, *I wish Dennis would kiss me like that.* I didn't want this relationship; I wanted this kind of relationship with Dennis.

George convinced me to meet him in the Jacuzzi after working out. I was nervous about him seeing me in a swimsuit, but I changed and met him at the indoor pool. As we sat in the very public Jacuzzi, we talked about "what might have been" if we had wound up together and then George started asking me to run away with him. He proposed that we could divorce our spouses and marry each other. I told him no repeatedly. I regularly reminded him that even the kind of talking we had been doing was wrong and a betrayal of our spouses. I really loved Dennis and wanted my marriage to succeed. I told him that I loved my four-year-old son and could never abandon him.

While I never considered leaving Dennis to be with George, and wasn't even tempted to do that, I did think I loved George at that point. And I wondered if we would have been a better match. I did not view George as "the one that got away" or someone who would have necessarily been the ideal husband. I knew enough to know I probably would not have been any happier if I had married him. I would just have different problems. However, I did ever so briefly entertain the notion that I might have brought out the best in him if he had married me. In hindsight, I realize that notion was just a part of the deception I was caught up in. After all, I hadn't exactly brought out the best in Dennis.

The next big mistake was agreeing to meet George at a park near his work—miles away from where we both lived. He called in sick and met me there. It felt safe to me because it was the middle of the day and there were people around. But it was definitely a romantic date, and another barrier came down. We walked around holding hands and talking. And then we sat on a blanket under a tree, and kissed. I was twenty-two years old and was behaving like a teenager making out with her boyfriend in the park. But I was doing this while married to someone else. I knew it was wrong, but I was so emotionally starved that I felt unable to resist. His words and attention were like water quenching my thirsty soul. Looking back it seems so ridiculous, but I agreed to a second park meeting the next week. I thought I could keep from taking our physical relationship any further because I was meeting him in broad daylight in a public place, but I was wrong.

The next week as I drove to the park there was a war going on in my heart and mind. I absolutely knew what I was doing was morally and spiritually wrong. I thought about the people I was betraying: George's wife, my husband, my son. I tried to rationalize my behavior theologically of all things. I had been taught that nobody makes it to heaven unless they first become perfect, and I mean literally by overcoming all sinfulness in the flesh. Being Jesus' equal here on earth. I was also taught there was no literal hell, just the grave. No matter how much I loved God or tried my best to live for Him, it would ultimately not matter unless I could reach perfection. If I did not "make it," I would just die and cease to exist—no difference between me and someone who fully rejected God. As I drove to the park I thought about the doctrine of perfection and how I would never be perfect or go to heaven anyway, so this life was basically all I had. And all I wanted was to be loved. Was that so bad? I wasn't killing anybody. What difference did it make? It certainly wasn't as if George and his wife had a good marriage. I imagined her being as miserable as he was. That wasn't my fault. And I had been mistreated in my marriage for years. God didn't seem to care a whole lot about that. So what difference did it make if I made the "right" choice when I could never be good enough to please God anyway? And how "fair" was it for Him to curse the whole human race and then expect any of us to be perfect? This was my frame of mind as I made one of the worst decisions of my life.

In no way do I make any excuses for my behavior. Although the physical act of adultery was not premeditated on my part, these meetings were. But I do want to explain that the justifications I was making in my own mind had a lot to do with my spiritual foundation. I did not know the Gospel of Jesus Christ. I did not know God's grace. I did not have the hope and promise of eternal life. And because my focus was entirely on myself and my inability to measure up to God's unreachable expectations, my focus was not on Jesus and what He had already done on my behalf. I had no hope. And I was able to turn that into self-pity, which enabled me to diminish the cries of my conscience and make it all about me and my emotional needs. As I look back from the perspective of today, I am most saddened by the reality that my obedience to God revolved around what was in it for me instead of honoring and loving Him.

George had suggested a different park. One I had never been to. This park was more remote and private than the first. I assume now that this was intentional on his part. When I pulled up George was waiting for me. We walked hand in hand to a secluded spot. I had convinced myself that I would never consummate our relationship. We sat on a blanket and talked. Physical lust did not lead me to that park or to George. I was emotionally invested in the relationship. But we started kissing and making out like before, and then in the moment I allowed it to go further. The romantic spell was instantly broken by the reality of what I had done. And the minute it was over, I was overcome with guilt, regret, and remorse. George began making plans to meet again, but I couldn't entertain the thought. He tried to convince me that since it had happened once, it didn't matter how many times it happened again. We were just as guilty whether it was one offense or many. I agreed and I disagreed. True, once is enough to be guilty. But I believed there was a difference between willful, planned sin and being "overtaken in a fault" (Galatians 6:1), as I had heard our pastor say many times. I'm not saying that because it was a sin of passion and weakness that somehow excuses or diminishes the wrong. I know my actions were selfish. I don't write it off casually as just a mistake. But I could not go forward with premeditated adultery. In my mind that would have been worse than what I had already done in the sight of God. And George said something that helped break the spell for me too. He asked if I had ever smoked marijuana to enhance sex. He wanted to introduce me to that experience. That grossed me out and made me feel cheap. His eagerness to use some kind of external enhancement made the relationship seem suddenly less emotional and all about the physical for him. I wasn't ever looking for a heightened sexual experience. Up until that moment, I had believed he loved me. I had also never tried marijuana and had no desire to. Nothing could have made him more unappealing in that moment. Being sheltered and naïve, what I didn't realize was that he wanted to lower my inhibitions chemically—though I do understand this in hindsight. And that is exploitation, certainly not love.

I cried all the way home, begging God to forgive me. I promised Him I would never let it happen again. And from that day forward, I passionately tried to be the perfect wife. I feared that if Dennis ever found out he would surely leave me. *Maybe, I thought, if I could make him happy he would know how remorseful I was and how much I wanted our marriage to survive.*

Not long after the park encounter, I met a friend at a restaurant after a church service and confessed what I had done. I told her how horribly guilty I felt. That I didn't know what to do and that George kept calling me and was making it difficult for me to end all contact. I told her that I never met him again and had told him it was over, but that he was still pursuing me and wouldn't take no for an answer. I knew I needed to confess to my pastor, Brother Mears, and seek his counsel, but I was afraid. My friend convinced me to go to Brother Mears' house that night.

Brother Mears' father-in-law had just died, and I knew his entire family was at his house that night. As much as I genuinely wanted to get this behind me, I felt conflicted about going right that minute. It was very late at night, and I didn't want to interrupt their family time in light of the sad circumstances. My friend insisted and even threatened to drag me there if I didn't agree to go willingly. I resisted her at first; it was an emotional moment. Even though I felt pressured and unsure of the timing, I still appreciate my friend for pushing me to do what we both believed was "the right thing" at the time.

When we got to Brother Mears' house, my friend told Sister Mears that we needed to see Brother Mears. Sister Mears led us into the living room where we waited. They lived in a large house. The kitchen and family room area could be closed off from the living and dining rooms, where Brother Mears could meet privately with people who needed to talk to him. I never saw the rest of the extended family, but I knew everyone was there. I could hear voices and activity. Staying up late was not unusual for their family, even under ordinary circumstances.

I will never forget sitting down on my pastor's living room sofa, crying and confessing my sin. I could not have been more embarrassed talking to my pastor about adultery; he was the same man who had shamed me for wearing lipstick, blush, and sleeves above my elbows. However, to my surprise, he demonstrated more mercy and compassion in that situation than he had on occasions when he thought I was wearing too much makeup. He was kind, gentle, and compassionate that night. He said that he could tell I had genuine godly sorrow and was repentant. He assured me that God would forgive and restore me. And then he gave me very bad advice. He told me it was not necessary to confess to my husband. He even *advised* me to keep it a secret and tell no one. He said it wasn't necessary for Dennis or George's wife to ever know. I had confessed and repented to God. And I had confessed and repented to him. God did not require me to confess and repent to my husband specifically.

Since my greatest fear was how Dennis would react, I felt some relief in being told by my pastor that God didn't require me to tell him. But it didn't feel right in my heart, and I didn't believe I could keep it a secret forever. Anyone who knows me knows that I am unusually quick to confess the smallest fault or misstep. As it turned out, it took less than six months for the secret to be uncovered.

Those six months were unbearable. I did everything in my power to please my husband and earn his future forgiveness by lavishing gratitude and attention on him, but I was racked with guilt. One night I had a vivid dream that caused me to wake up crying and groaning. Dennis thought I had just had a random nightmare. Well, it was a nightmare all right, but it wasn't random. I dreamed that everyone had found out what I had done and decided my punishment was to be buried alive. In my dream, Dennis and my dad were forcing me into a coffin. I was crying hysterically and begging for my life. The coffin wasn't even long enough for my body, and I was scrunched painfully into it. I kept telling them it was too small. I begged for forgiveness but they only shook their heads, united in their mutual disgust for me as they began to close the lid. Then I woke up sweating.

The secret was revealed in January of 1982. Dennis had just been released from the hospital following gall bladder surgery. I received a phone call from George's wife. She told me that she needed to talk to me in person, and if I cared anything about her I would come there immediately and tell her the truth. She knew. I made some excuse to Dennis about my "friend" needing to talk to me and went to her house. My pastor was out of town, so I had no one to go to for guidance. It was raining hard that day, and I remember thinking as I drove that it felt like I was in a scene from a bad movie. It felt like my life was shattering. The fear was almost suffocating.

At her house we sat down at the kitchen table. I answered every question honestly. I acknowledged the wrong and asked her forgiveness, adding that I did not deserve it. She responded that she didn't know if she would ever be able to forgive me. (Ultimately she and her family did extend forgiveness to me. And I was humbled and grateful to receive it.) She was not cruel to me that day. In fact, I thought she was pretty calm under the circumstances. Her questions humiliated me, but I believed she was entitled to have answers.

She told me that she wasn't ever going to tell anyone and neither would anyone in her family. She said it was my choice whether or not to tell Dennis. I knew I had to tell him. I could not take the chance that he would ever hear it from someone other than me. I went home and faced his wrath.

When I told Dennis he lit into me with some horrible insults and accusations. He verbally humiliated me, but he did not lay a hand on me. It was one of the few times I felt like his anger was justified. I took my medicine and begged his forgiveness. He packed some things and left me there with his sister (who had been living with us temporarily). It was an awkward and uncomfortable few days since his sister was upset with me as well. Dennis came home for a little while, but he was conflicted about what to do. We began a six-month-long period of separating and getting back together. (It was during these six months that he walked up behind me in the kitchen and *jokingly* choked me.) During the six months we were trying to work through this, he went to George's house one day and physically attacked George. He boasted of breaking his jaw and his nose. And I'll never forget how our pastor reacted. He asked Dennis if he felt better now. Dennis said he did and he would not have to do anything like that again. At the end of those six months Dennis finally said he could forgive me and that he actually wished he could get past it and stay married, but he couldn't. He felt I had publicly humiliated him and that was the part he couldn't live with. He felt like everyone who looked at him was feeling sorry for him. In August he filed for divorce.

He not only left me, he left the church. For a year and a half he proceeded to get even with me and life. He had several affairs with married women. I think only two of his girlfriends during that time were single. One of the married women was the beautiful college girlfriend he had called back in 1977 when he was drunk. Our divorce was final on March 3, 1983.

At the beginning of 1984, Dennis began coming to church again and trying to convince me to go out to dinner with him. By this time, I felt like I was over him and had moved on. I was not interested in going out with him. In fact, I rudely refused his request, but he was tenacious. We had joint custody of Danny and had regular phone conversations concerning drop-offs and pick-ups. We were cordial enough during the calls and the meetings. One evening we were making plans for Danny on the phone, and Dennis interjected that Brother Mears believed we should get back together. I laughed and told him he needed to tell Brother Mears that that was never going to happen. Dennis was unfazed and continued his sales pitch. He told me that he took full responsibility for what I'd done and knew that if he had not been a total jerk of a husband, I never would have fallen into that situation. He said he had been involved with several married women, and now he understood how vulnerable a neglected woman could be. He told me that he had thought it would be easy to replace me with someone new, but his dating and affairs had made him realize that I had all the qualities he was looking for in a woman. He said he had met women with perhaps one of my qualities, but none with all of them. His words were very kind, conciliatory, and affirming. I believed they were coming from his heart. I didn't think I was being conned or manipulated. But I was still reluctant and apprehensive. I *really* did not want to be with him again.

He was persistent. My discouragement did not deter him. He finally convinced me to just have dinner with him once. He took me to a restaurant I had always loved and spent the entire evening reinforcing what a good person I was and how wrong it had been that he'd walked away and let me go through the public humiliation alone. He thanked me for being the parent who continued to take Danny to church, even though church was one of the hardest places for me to be. He acknowledged that I had forgiven him so many times, hiding all of his bad behavior and protecting his reputation, but he had dumped me when I needed his forgiveness. He was charming, and he said all the right things. He asked if I could forgive him and give him the chance to make it up to me. He said, "If you will give me the chance, I know I can make you happy. I will spend the rest of my life making you happy. I promise."

I had such strong reservations, but he was finally giving me what I had always craved—validation, affirmation, value—and it was breaking down a barrier, softening me up. I was also scared because I knew how bad it had been and how bad it could be again. When we had initially separated, I was more than happy to blame myself 100 percent for the affair. I told everyone it was my fault, and he was a good husband. In no way could he be blamed even a little bit for what I had done.

When Dennis first started trying to win me back I responded harshly. "When you needed my forgiveness, I forgave you and protected you. When I needed your forgiveness, you dumped me and let me take the fall. Well, guess what? I don't need your forgiveness anymore." If I had said something like that to him during our first marriage, he would have responded in anger. But because he was so desperate to get back together, he validated my sentiments. He said he understood my feelings and that I was right. He was determined to do whatever it took to prove to me that he had really changed. Despite my boldness I doubted that I was right to take that kind of control.

Self-doubt and self-contempt had been my auto-pilot, and even more after my moral failure. I didn't know there was a term for the way I felt about myself. I was experiencing toxic-shame. I focused exclusively on what was wrong with me instead of any wrong Dennis had done. And I focused on how deserving I was of punishment. I was programmed for this. Dennis had manipulated me into thinking I was always the guilty one since I was sixteen years old. My dad had always told me to take my punishment on the chin and not try to let myself off the hook by making excuses. I was raised to be hard on myself. And then I was beaten down mentally and emotionally by Dennis.

Long before I had an affair Dennis would make me *pay* even for small offenses. I had to be humble and sorry, and grateful when he decided to get over something, so being humble came naturally. Because Dennis had actually been nicer to me around the time I was unfaithful, I had convinced myself that my affair had nothing to do with how he had treated me. I blamed myself completely and doubted my worth in the process. In my mind, I had messed up royally right when things were probably about to get better. I shared with a few people what the marriage actually had been like, but I still didn't want to blame him for my choices. I have always had a strong conviction that when I screw up and do the wrong thing, I need to "face the music" as my dad would say. I didn't want to rationalize or excuse my actions, so I went to the opposite extreme. Even after I knew God had forgiven me, I continued to beat up on myself. I would call myself names like adulteress. My closest friends urged me to stop talking about myself that way. They were right. It was self-destructive, but I felt as if I had to *prove* to people how sorry I was. One friend at church pleaded with me to stop being so hard on myself by saying, "Shari, nobody is wanting you to lie on the altar and bleed to prove you're repentant." But not cutting myself any slack was drilled into me as a child, and Dennis continued to be hard on me after we were married. I thought I was simply owning the wrong, but I am finally able to label all of this for what it was: toxic shame.

From that first date, it only took six weeks for Dennis to convince me to remarry him. I prayed about it and was convinced in my heart that it was God's will. I had been taught that since I was guilty of adultery, I could never be free to remarry anyone but Dennis. I was only twenty-four years old. I didn't believe I was capable of remaining single for the rest of my life. *What were the chances that someone as weak as me would be able to live single for the rest of my life?* I thought. I concluded that perhaps it was God's mercy; God's way of giving me another shot at a normal life. I thought that if it was God's will for me, then surely I would be happy. I'm not sure why I thought that, since I hadn't ever believed my happiness mattered to God before.

My dad was outspokenly opposed to the marriage. He finally gave up and said, "Well, I guess you're at least going into it already knowing the worst about him." I remember going out to his office behind the house and asking if he wanted to go with us to the ceremony. He declined.

My spiritual beliefs played a significant role in my decision to go back to my ex-husband. It also made me happy to see the gleam in my young son's eyes. We were remarried on March 17, 1984. And shortly thereafter, Danny told us that the reason we were back together was because he had prayed.

For a while, I was truly happy. Dennis was treating me as if I had value for the first time. My son had his parents together again. And I believed God had restored me. I allowed myself to believe that our second marriage would never resemble our first. My hopes were high for the future. No matter what happened, though, I believed it was a fresh start. I was glad that Dennis had divorced me instead of forgiving me because it meant I had already "paid" for wronging him. He insisted he would never bring it up again, but I must have doubted him because I remember thinking: *At least he can never use that against me in this marriage.*

My self-doubt was temporarily eased.

Chapter 5
A Frog in Hot Water

"Why would anyone choose, repeatedly and perpetually, to offer him or herself as fuel for another's consuming need for inflation, and at such a price? Why would someone sacrifice Self so completely for "love"? The nickel answer to this question is that he or she has been programmed to self-effacement and self-abasement by earlier life experiences." —Sandy Hotchkiss

THE FIRST YEAR OF REMARRIAGE WAS QUITE GOOD. I would have described myself as blissfully happy that first year. I'm not sure that someone who had never been abused would have been as happy as I was, though. After living the way I had lived previously, the bar was set low. But I remember feeling that God had been merciful to me. I wasn't the only one who looked at it this way. I will never forget sitting in Brother Mears' living room just before we remarried. Dennis and I were discussing reconciliation with Brother Mears when he looked at me rather sternly (in what had been a happy moment up to then) and informed me that Brother Dennis was being merciful to me by taking me back and I should be thankful. I felt completely invalidated by his words. Despite the abuse I had endured, and the numerous affairs Dennis had confessed to with married women, Brother Mears seemed to view me as the person needing all the forgiveness and mercy. Dennis was physically involved with the first girlfriend during the six months he was still vacillating between forgiving me and leaving me. Brother Mears was fully aware of that because Dennis questioned him about his freedom being "in jeopardy."

He vacillated back and forth, dating her during our brief separations, then coming back home to me until he left again and resumed dating her. I was also fully aware of her at the time and thought maybe he needed to even the score for the sake of his wounded pride. He told me he was physically involved with her when he wasn't with me. But it was like Brother Mears gave him a grace period for making up his mind, and it didn't matter that he was with other women during that time. When he filed for divorce, Dennis boasted to me that Brother Mears assured him he was "still free" to remarry and that his sins didn't free me. It didn't seem fair or unbiased, but it was consistent with everything I'd ever been taught.

That's how it was where I grew up. It was denied that men were regarded more highly than women, but they were. I knew that Dennis hadn't lied to me, since Brother Mears told me himself that I was forever bound to Dennis (never free to marry anyone else) because of my sin, but that Dennis was completely free. It was a hard pill to swallow. During the year that we were divorced, I began to feel deep regret over having protected Dennis and his reputation all throughout our marriage. It probably wouldn't have made a difference in my status as far as my pastor was concerned, but I felt I had no one to blame other than myself for keeping the abuse hidden. To Dennis' credit he did change early in our second marriage. He did treat me better for a while. He even had his vasectomy reversed at one point so we could try to have another child. The reversal failed, and I've always believed it was a blessing in disguise.

They say a frog will jump out if dropped into a kettle of scalding water. But if you put it in warm water and slowly turn up the heat, the frog will sit there and die. Well, like a frog in a pot of warm water, I did not jump out of the relationship the second time around, and the temperature did begin to rise.

We were remarried in March of 1984 and I can't put a date on when I started to realize the second "honeymoon" was over. It was before my mom was diagnosed with colon cancer in November of 1986. Dennis began to revert back to his old behaviors of belittling and demeaning me. It was gradual, like a pot of water being brought to a boil. Dennis continued to battle depression and bi-polar mood swings. There were lots of highs and lows, but I took the lows in stride pretty well. I have a vivid memory of Danny coming out of his bedroom, blowing loudly and wildly on his trumpet during one of our arguments. Our fighting was upsetting him and that was his way of demanding that we stop. His reaction made me realize just how much my son was suffering emotionally from our problems.

൞

When Dennis was trying to win me back, I made it clear to him that if he ever hit me again, I would leave. I would not put up with physical violence. He promised he would never again lay a hand on me in anger. He acknowledged the past physical abuse, and that was a big factor in my willingness to take him back. If he had denied abusing me that way or tried to minimize it, I would not have remarried him. He not only acknowledged it, he repented and promised he would never behave that way again.

However, it didn't take long for his manipulation to start. After we'd been remarried only a year or so, he started trying to convince me that the violence hadn't really happened the way I remembered. He would make subtle references as if he was trying to influence my memory or get me to agree that maybe it hadn't happened the way I remembered it. While we were broken up Dennis had dated a woman who was the daughter of one of my dad's friends in the church. My dad had warned his friend about Dennis' temper. After we were remarried Dennis was bragging to me that the woman had wanted to marry him—which I later found out wasn't true—and had asked him about his temper. Dennis said, "I told her that wasn't true and your dad was making it up to make me look bad. I was surprised your dad would stoop to that. You know I wasn't violent with you." I felt myself tense up inside as he said this so casually and matter-of-factly. It felt like a test. I would not agree. I challenged him on it.

"You really don't remember being physical with me in our first marriage?" He rolled his eyes and shook his head dismissively as if I was delusional.

He became more aggressive in challenging my memory. "Come on, Shari. You and I both know your dad blew it out of proportion. I never hurt you. And the times our fights escalated into a push or a slap were few and far between." Now he was trying to intimidate me into agreeing with him. I didn't back down and I was proud of myself for standing firm. When he realized that I was not going to agree to his version of the past, he just dropped it. I had anticipated this might escalate into a fight, but instead he changed the subject.

In retrospect, now that I have studied these psychological behavior patterns, I have to wonder if he was trying to reject the shame he felt by denying the past. But denying the abuse was not an option for me. If that's what it took to pacify him, I wasn't willing to cooperate.

I had gotten stronger as a person since our first marriage. I knew if I ever gave the slightest indication that perhaps it wasn't that bad (out of compassion and kindness), it would be used against me as a weapon. The enabling part of me at times wanted to let him off the hook because I didn't want him to carry guilt over wrongs for which he had already repented. But I just could not bring myself to participate in his denial of reality. We had a few heated exchanges about it, but I never backed down. And then he just dropped it. Unlike in our first marriage I finally was able to stand up to him.

When my mom was diagnosed with terminal cancer in late 1986, Dennis was supportive and unselfish. We lived around the corner from my parents during this terrible time, and I was completely consumed with being the best daughter I could be when my mom needed me most. Everything else in my life took a back seat, including Dennis and Danny. When someone is dying of cancer and you are one of the primary caregivers, everything else in life becomes less significant. Dennis was more than willing for my life to revolve around my mother and her needs for the entire seven months. Those were some of his best moments as a husband. And I have to give him credit for that. He did love my mother very much.

It still puzzles me in hindsight how this same man could almost be two different people. He was the meanest person I have ever experienced. He bullied, belittled, demeaned, and abused me the majority of the years I spent with him. But there was also a heart inside the monster. He was capable of kindness and generosity. He was witty and could be a lot of fun when he was in a good mood. There were even brief windows of humility and repentance, but he always allowed his dark side to overwhelm his potential for growth in a positive direction. My son has always said it this way, "Dad would have fought anyone who tried to hurt you, *except himself.*"

After Dennis' passing, I learned things I never knew including very damaging, blatant lies Dennis told during our marriage. I never viewed him as a pathological liar, but I now think he was. He told his family that my dad sexually molested me; made up a scenario describing said abuse and claimed I was the one who told him it happened. In all those years, I never knew he'd said any such thing; yet he made this claim early in our first marriage and never corrected the falsehood. To say I was shocked at learning this would be an understatement. I experienced a level of betrayal greater than any I had ever experienced in all the years Dennis was alive. I cannot fathom how anyone could make up something so destructive about another person. And for the first time, I realized I didn't know him as well as I thought I did. I will probably never know who else he said such things to—about me, about my family. And I don't need to. But since I have the opportunity to do so here, I definitely want to set the record straight. That story was a disgusting fabrication without even a shred of truth to it. And I never made such a claim to Dennis or anyone else.

୨

Life began to get rocky again after my mom passed away. The heat was being turned up. There was a lot of family stress around the time of my mom's death. Tragedy does not always bring out the best in people, and it felt like my family fractured with her death.

My mother was terminally ill for seven months, and I devoted myself to caring for her. Other family members were pitching in to help as well, but I was trying to do as much of the care giving as I possibly could. My mother and I weren't shopping buddies like a lot of moms and daughters are. We had not been extremely close, and suddenly I was faced with a limited amount of time with her. I not only needed to be in her presence, but I needed to demonstrate to her how much I loved her and how important she was to me. I wanted to be the world's best daughter in those circumstances. I wanted my mom to have no doubts whatsoever that her care was my highest priority. So I did as much as I could possibly do to prove my love and devotion.

I had always felt like I wore the label of the black sheep because I didn't try as hard as my brother Todd did to comply with our parents' expectations. I was outspoken and resisted my parents' expectations of me. I'm sure there were parts of my personality that were a challenge for them. I wanted to be loved for who I was, not for being who they wanted me to be. And I may have even had a chip on my shoulder about that, but when my mom was dying I was consumed by my need for her (and my dad's) love, validation, and approval. No doubt about that.

My dad was making wrong assumptions about the motivation behind my desire to be with my mother round the clock. He thought I was trying to take control of the situation. He thought I was trying to exclude Sue, my sister-in-law, or anyone else from helping care for my mother. That definitely wasn't what I was trying to do. Wanting to be with Mom all the time had nothing to do with being in control of anything for me. Control could not have been further from my thoughts. I was losing my mother and wanted to spend as much time with her as I could before she passed. More than once in the afternoons Sue had shown up and offered to relieve me so I could go shopping or take a break, but I didn't want to leave because nothing seemed as important to me as just being in the same room with my mother for as many days or weeks as I had left to be in her presence. What my dad didn't know was that as she got worse Mom had asked Grandma and I (at least one of us) to stay with her all the time. She didn't want both of us to leave the house. She didn't seem to want to tell anyone else that, as far as I knew, for fear of hurting their feelings. However, recently I was able to have a heart-to-heart talk with my sister-in-law, Sue, about these events. Our conversation was so healing for me. She shared with me that she *knew* Mom wanted me because Mom had said to her, "Sue, you know I love you, but Shari is my daughter." Sue told me that Mom said it as though she thought she had to apologize for wanting her daughter by her side, but that she understood and it didn't upset her. I was so grateful that Sue shared those words with me; even this many years later, it was a gift that gave me such peace. I'm still not sure Mom ever shared her feelings with my dad, though.

My mom loved my dad so much. And she could see that her illness and impending death were tearing him apart. She knew him better than anybody, and she sensed he was angry. Truth was he was angry at God, but he took it out on me. He took me aside one morning and solemnly said, "When Todd married Sue, she became our daughter. I love her as much as I love you. No difference to me that you are my flesh and blood. And you need to know that if there's ever a problem between the two of you, I will never take your side just because you're my daughter. Is that understood?"

I was thinking his words and timing were so bizarre, but my dad is known for sometimes saying inappropriate things. I didn't want to have any conflict with him or anyone else. So I calmly responded, "Dad, I already know this. But Sue and I don't have a problem." And I really believed that.

Much later in the afternoon or early evening, Elaine, a close friend of my mom's, called from Phoenix. She desperately wanted to come see my mom and help take some of the load off of Grandma and me. Dennis and Danny had stopped by the house and were sitting in the family room with my dad as he was shaking his head no and telling me he didn't want her there. I didn't know why he objected to her coming so much, since she had always been a close friend of the family. But I was trying to discourage her to avoid upsetting him. I kept saying we were fine and we could manage. But she kept insisting. Well, ultimately I made the mistake of saying, "Okay. If you really want to...."

When my dad heard me say this, he got visibly angry and complained loudly, "She won't even *let* Sue come down and help, but she's inviting Elaine to come?!"

Dennis sprung to my defense, "Jerry! How can you say that? Shari hasn't tried to keep Sue from helping. That's ridiculous."

"Oh, you think *your wife* is so lily white. Well, let me tell you, she's not. There's a lot that you don't know."

"How can you treat your daughter this way? Shari has been here day in and day out, sometimes all night long, taking care of Jane, taking care of you and this house, doing laundry, cooking meals. And this is how you thank her for that?"

I walked out of the family room and stood around the corner in the hallway. I couldn't bear to be in the same room and see the hostility in my dad's eyes as he talked this way about me, his own daughter. But what he said next devastated me.

"Ah! The *only* reason Shari is here taking care of Jane is because she knows it's all the stress she caused her mother that gave Jane cancer in the first place!"

I dissolved into tears. I was crushed. But I was also angry. I charged back into the room and announced to my dad: "As long as my mother is breathing, you are going to have to put up with my presence here. I'm not leaving her side for anybody, including you. But after she's gone, you won't have to worry about me darkening your door after what you just said." Even as the words left my lips I knew that my dad's accusation wasn't about me. It was about my dad. He carried a lot of guilt for being a stressful *husband* to live with. He needed to get that guilt off of his back and onto someone else. I was the convenient someone else. My dad insisted Dennis leave and, out of respect for my mom, Dennis left willingly rather than going toe to toe with my father.

Mom was admitted to the hospital to get her medication regulated. She went into a coma and died within the week. Dennis stayed away so he would not contribute to any unnecessary family tension after the ugly scene with my dad in the family room. I remember standing in that hospital room with my dad, Todd and Sue, and my grandmother, feeling like an outcast.

I worked hard at rising above the pain. I was at my mother's bedside every day in the hospital. At the visitation I desperately hoped my dad would apologize and make amends. He did not say he was sorry, but he said that he wished it hadn't happened and he hoped everything could just go back to the way it was before the argument. I hugged him and told him I loved him. Dennis shook his hand, but it was much harder for him to forgive. He thought he was in competition with my family for my allegiance, and this gave him fire power, a weapon against my family for many years to come. His resentment of my dad and Todd fueled many heated arguments behind closed doors. I suffered the most because I wanted to be at peace with both my husband and my family. I am, by nature, a forgiving person and that was a continual irritation to Dennis when it came to my family. Dennis held grudges. And Dennis was uncomfortable with emotions that made him feel weak. He channeled all his "weak feeling" emotions—hurt, disappointment, and sadness—into anger. It camouflaged his weakness with a false sense of empowerment. When I was hurt, he wanted me to be angry like he was and react the way he did. His angry outbursts always embarrassed me, and I had no desire to react the way he did. He would berate me for trying to do the right thing where my family was concerned, and the family stress contributed to the heat being turned up on me at home.

In 1990 my dad remarried and many friends and family members had reservations about his new wife. I was willing to try to have a relationship with her, but I wanted it to evolve naturally. I wasn't going to put on a display of affection at church to demonstrate a false unity among our family. Acting as Dad's advocate, my brother asked me for a show of support, and I honestly shared my conflicting emotions and reservations. Dad and Todd have always been very close as father and son. Todd had his back. I didn't. I told Todd that pretending to have affection I didn't yet feel seemed wrong to me. I have always been uncomfortable with insincerity. My unwillingness to cooperate fueled new tensions between Dad and me. To make matters worse, someone was telling Dad that I was spreading rumors to others to besmirch his new wife's reputation. We were estranged for a year and a half. Dad felt wronged by me and I felt unfairly forsaken by my dad.

In 1991, in the middle of my estrangement with my dad, my new stepmother decided to host my youngest sister-in-law's baby shower at my dad's house. Dennis was livid. He said it was thoughtless and showed complete contempt for me, as well as a disregard for my feelings of discomfort. He believed it was an intentional jab, and insisted that I not attend (even though my dad would not be present at the shower). He said refusing to go was the *right* thing to do. I disagreed and told him I was capable of rising above my discomfort and that I would not allow anyone to make me so uncomfortable that I would miss out on such an important family occasion. He wouldn't budge. I tried to get him to see that he was doing the very thing he was mad at them for. He was showing contempt and a disregard for my feelings by insisting I not go. We had several heated battles over this, and it was the first time in our second marriage that I saw Dennis' rage turn physical. He did not strike me, but he got so frustrated with my refusal to bow to his will that he walked over to my exercise bike *while I was riding it* and shook it hard, picking up the front end and slamming it down on the floor as he yelled at me. Then he stormed out of the room and slammed the door. This was how far downhill his behavior had plummeted. The water was simmering.

Dennis finally simmered down and life went on. My dad and I weren't speaking for about a year and a half when I started to feel a tug on my heart. It wasn't about being a good daughter. It was about my sincerity as a Christian. I felt that our relationship was not reflecting the love of God to anyone, let alone each other, and it bothered me. I went through a repeat performance of the same outrage from Dennis after I shared with him that I felt God wanted me to choose humility and try to mend things with my dad and his wife. One day I decided to stop by their house unannounced to ask their forgiveness for hurting them and for anything I had unknowingly done to contribute to our estrangement. I was sincere, and to my surprise their response was warm. We sat down and talked, and they also asked my forgiveness. That encounter resulted in genuine reconciliation. I didn't want to offer a generic apology (*if* I've done anything to offend), but I honestly didn't know exactly what I had done and needed to make right. That had been part of the hurt resulting from my dad's rejection. So I asked my dad and his wife to tell me specifically what I had done to hurt them so I could understand and *genuinely* ask their forgiveness. As a result of my question, we were able to clear up some of the false assumptions my dad had made regarding things he thought I had said and done. For some reason he believed I had contacted old friends of his to say negative things about his wife so they would not accept her. (How he arrived at this conclusion is a mystery because he admitted nobody had accused me of that.) I told him I had not spoken to his friends. Then he told me that the pastor's daughter (someone I had thought of as a friend) had made an accusation about me treating her unkindly, which my dad believed. The interaction he relayed to me didn't happen the way she described it. And I was shocked, not only that she would make up a story to put me in a bad light but that my dad would believe her without even asking me if it were true. These discoveries helped me understand his anger better. He said he believed me and apologized to me for misjudging me. Had I not initiated this conversation, my dad would have gone on believing I was guilty of deliberately trying to hurt him and others.

I had gone to my dad's house that day without consulting Dennis first, knowing that he would not support me in following my own conviction. I hoped he would at least be happy that it had gone well and I felt better. Of course, Dennis was not happy about the outcome. He was upset with me for making the first step to reach out to them regardless of the outcome. He insisted that they should have been the ones to seek my forgiveness. He said I had rewarded them for mistreating me and viewed it as my choosing my family over him. But that wasn't true. I was trying to follow Christ.

In hindsight, I don't know if God was actually requiring this of me. But I never regretted my decision. I had based my actions on the admonition of Matthew 5:23-24, to go to your brother or sister and be reconciled to them if you know they have something against you. God blessed my efforts, allowing me to reap the love I had sown. And I regained a relationship with my dad. There was a price to pay, though, for my noncompliance to Dennis' wishes. I suffered at home for my decision. Like that frog in the water, I was feeling the heat of the simmering pot, but outweighing the wrath of Dennis was the inner peace of believing I had honored and pleased God.

Chapter 6
THE HOLES IN OUR HEARTS

"Yes, Mother. I can see you are flawed. You have not hidden it. That is your greatest gift to me." —Alice Walker

I BELIEVE GOD CREATED US WITH A NEED TO BE *KNOWN* as well as loved. My parents did not know who I was on the inside and it constantly hurt me. We are all flawed and fragile in some way. It's part of the human condition. Some of my flaws were caused by deep-seated needs that weren't met by my parents or those in authority over me when I was young. Consequentially, I have emotional holes in my heart that were formed during my most formative years. My holes are filled by reassurances of love, acceptance, and value from others. Someone else (like Dennis) may seek to fill their holes through a sense of superiority and control over others to compensate for feelings of weakness and inadequacy. Of course, the only remedy for the holes in our hearts is found in our relationship with God, not in other people.

Dennis was a fragile person. If you knew him, this might make you chuckle because he was a very large guy. But his physical strength was not an indicator of his emotional strength. Men who bully the way Dennis bullied are the weakest and most insecure men in the entire world. Strong men do not bully others, especially women. But weak men cover up their feelings of inadequacy and neediness by overcompensating with aggression and intimidation, always trying to display their superiority. Inside, though, they actually feel anything but superior. I saw that in Dennis. I want to make it clear that I am not excusing his abusive behavior. As Lundy Bancroft points out, in *Why Does He Do That?* "An abuser can seem emotionally needy. You can get caught in a trap of catering to him, trying to fill a bottomless pit. But he's not so much needy as entitled, so no matter how much you give him, it will never be enough. He will just keep coming up with more demands because he believes his needs are your responsibility, until you feel drained down to nothing." That is why I felt torn as a victim. If you love the man who is abusing you and care about his emotional needs, you will feel compelled to try constantly to meet them. And often the underlying issue is really a grandiose sense of entitlement.

∾

Dennis and I had a similar past, but we responded in different ways to some of the same spiritual abuses. Dennis grew up attending a church in Ohio that was affiliated with the church I grew up in. I believe he was in the fourth grade when his family moved to Southern California. His mom had been urged to find Brother Mears' church in San Gabriel when they got settled. And they did. I don't remember his family that far back. I was six and a half years younger than Dennis, but apparently we attended church together when I was a little girl.

Dennis' father left his mother for another woman when she was thirty-nine years old. Dennis was in high school. His older brother was going away to college and his younger sister was four years old when the family faced this crisis. His dad died tragically of electrocution before I ever met him, but I remember his mom often referring to her ex-husband as "that dirty dog." The pain he had caused her was still apparent even after decades had passed. I never heard her say that she forgave him. As a result of the pain she endured, she cautioned Dennis when he began to date not to let anyone hurt him. He shared with me that her warning was always in his mind even when it came to friendships. He knew that he would always be the first to push someone away if he thought they might hurt or reject him. I think that gave him a false sense of control. Unfortunately, it also robs you of any depth in your relationships because there is always a chance you will be hurt if you love and trust people. Deciding never to let anyone in enough to hurt you is a terribly self-destructive choice, but that was truly the way he lived.

Dennis' first signs of depression surfaced as a teenager. He had a tremendous amount of emotional pressure on him. He told me he felt responsible for the emotional welfare of his mother at all times. One of the saddest things he ever told me was that, when he was just a teenager, his mother kept a slip of paper with the suicide hotline phone number on her nightstand. She knew that slip of paper was visible to her son. She made no attempt to hide it. He would push his mom out the door on Saturday mornings and tell her to go shop yard sales (an activity she loved) while he cleaned the house for her. He believed that if he did things to "cheer her up" she might not kill herself. He felt that her very will to live rested on his young shoulders.

She made the decision to never remarry or pursue another relationship with a man. Instead, she chose to make her children her life. She lived through them. One of the biggest problems with this is that a mother who chooses to make her children her whole life often expects her children to return the favor. The behavior goes beyond neediness. It is demanding. And I personally experienced this side of my former mother-in-law many times.

She was an "overly involved" mother. And an overly involved mother is often the mother of a narcissist. Sadly, Dennis' mom had her own history of abuse. And there were holes in *her* heart that needed to be filled. One of the stories she told me many times was how her mother told her at a young age, "I will love my *boys* as long as breath warms my body." It was a cruel thing for a mother to say to her only daughter and she never recovered from it. She recalled those words many times in conversation with me. It was quite obvious she did not feel her mother's love growing up. Perhaps this contributed to her going to the other extreme with her own children. One thing I have learned in life is that there are always underlying reasons for our behaviors. We are all wounded people in some way or another. We all have holes in our hearts that we are trying to fill.

My former mother-in-law died in 1997. I had been her daughter-in-law for over twenty years. Initially she was thrilled for Dennis to marry me. But almost immediately after I joined the family, she acted as though I were a threat to her. She saw me as her rival where Dennis was concerned. She would frequently make remarks to Dennis about his loyalty to her. She reminded him that family is blood. One time she confided something in him concerning his younger sister, adding, "Don't tell Shari. We need to keep this in the family." Dennis did tell me the secret, as well as his mother's remark about keeping me out of the loop. I was extremely hurt because I thought I *was* a member of the family.

Dennis was caught between his mother and his wife as long as his mother was alive. Not because I put him in that position but because his mother needed constant reassurance that she was the most important person in his life. Perhaps this stemmed from not feeling like she was important to her own mother. But

I did not view her as a rival. In fact, being young and naïve and so eager to please, I tried to do everything in my power to win her over and make her like me in our early years. But all my groveling ever seemed to accomplish was giving her more power over me. She exploited my desire for a good relationship just like her son did. She would have me go in and pay overdue bills for her (to save her the embarrassment) and other unpleasant tasks. It became a running joke, and I laughed along with them, that I was "doing Mom's dirty work." I was trying to earn my value. After all, I just wanted to be loved and accepted. I would have done just about anything to gain her approval.

Like me, many people try to fill holes in their hearts with the approval of others. If you're doing that now, I hope you'll see how unhealthy it is and stop. I learned much too late in life that people who love you won't use and exploit you. My former mother-in-law frequently pitted Dennis against me in manipulative ways, and in his desire to please his mom, he enabled her. One night in particular stands out to me.

I enjoy nurturing others and always have, and one way I do that is by cooking for people. When people think of me, they think of food. It was not uncommon for me to invite Dennis' mother over for dinner. On this particular occasion, I made a big Mexican feast. Like her son, she preferred to sit in the living room with her plate on her lap, watching television as she ate. I cooked the meal. I served Dennis and his mom, taking their plates to them and then taking them back to the kitchen when they finished. Neither of them had to move from their chairs the whole evening. I cleaned up the kitchen by myself. I took them dessert and cleared those dishes as well. And I was glad to do it. They were both happy and full and everything was good. I then sat down on the couch to watch television with them. I was tired and wound up dozing off during *The Tonight Show*.

After a while I woke up feeling groggy. They were still watching television, so without giving it a second thought, I got up and went to bed. I didn't say anything to either of them.

When I got up the next morning, Dennis gave me a nasty look as if I should know I had done something wrong, but I was absolutely clueless. When I'd fallen asleep, everybody was happy. I asked, "What's wrong?"

"You were rude to my mother," he replied.

"What? I waited on her the whole night! How in the world was I rude?"

I will never forget his next sentence because it was so dramatic and over the top. "That poor woman was in tears last night because you got up and left the room without even saying goodnight to her."

That was the manipulation I grew to accept as my lot in life. Dennis had a love/hate relationship with his mother. On the one hand, he was controlled and manipulated by her, always seeking her approval. On the other, he deeply resented her for making him responsible for "cheering her up" his whole life and being appointed her emotional caretaker. He declared so many times that he would never do that to his son. But he wound up doing exactly the same thing to Danny, and he never seemed to see that in himself, right up to his death.

I was so desperate for peace and harmony that I agreed to apologize to my mother-in-law. She would stop speaking to me any time she felt offended no matter how trivial and petty the perceived offense. It was always my responsibility to patch things up. When she was mad at both of us, she'd take her phone off the hook. There were many times when Dennis would tell me that I didn't do anything wrong but would ask me to go to his mom and apologize just so she would answer her phone. (It was the complete opposite of what he expected of me when it came to my own family.) And I always complied. I bent over backwards to get along with her. Despite all her games and manipulations and challenges, I loved her. I tried to look behind her behavior to her wounds. Compassion helped me to forgive from my heart.

※

My mother-in-law also had a lot of fears and superstitions that she handed down to Dennis. When Dennis was a kid their house had burned down. She told him it was because they'd been playing cards the night before. She probably wanted to discourage him from gambling and card playing, but those kinds of fear-based warnings seriously damaged his view of God. Dennis believed that if you broke a rule, God would do something bad to you. And his fears ruled our house. For instance, Danny and I were not allowed to open a fortune cookie in a Chinese restaurant ever. He saw the movie *The Exorcist* when he was in college and was sent into a dark depression. It caused him to come back to church. (Dennis was always leaving and returning to church depending on his emotional state.) From then on Dennis had a fear of anything associated with the occult or the supernatural. He would frequently ask me to verify that I never read my horoscope. When the song "Aquarius" by The Fifth Dimension came on the radio, he would immediately change the channel. He associated his bouts of depression with wrongdoing and the occult.

He had notebooks filled with the phrase "no promises or vows" that he wrote repeatedly during church services. He was terrified of making a promise to God and not keeping it, so he had to remind himself in writing that he wasn't making any promises to God. I didn't know what rumination was back then. I thought his fears were strange, but I complied with Dennis' requests to the best of my ability.

In all the years I knew her, my former mother-in-law went to church only sporadically, but she was fiercely loyal to Brother Mears and the church. Dennis followed in her footsteps. For most of our married life he did not go to church or participate in church activities. He stayed home and watched television while I went with Danny. Our church had four services a week. Sometimes I went faithfully to every service. Other times, my attendance could be described as hit and miss, but I never stopped going completely until long after we had moved to Tennessee.

When Dennis was going to church, he was all in. When he wasn't going, he was all out. During those "all out" times Brother Mears was frequently sending Dennis messages through me. Dennis would often make caustic remarks in response. He seemed to feel no guilt for anything he said or did when not attending church. But when he would return to church (often because of fear and the onset of a depressive episode), he would shift into the opposite extreme. He would feel overly guilty about everything. His fears took on a life of their own. You couldn't disagree with Brother Mears around him, and we had to follow every rule. The strangest part was how he would become much more obsessed with controlling Danny's and my behavior than his own.

One day in the late eighties when we were still living in Southern California, we were looking forward to a day at Disneyland with Danny and his best buddy Matthew. I was getting ready and Dennis noticed I was wearing jeans, which was okay with him when he wasn't "in church." At this time, though, he was going, so it wasn't okay. (It was against church rules for women to wear pants.) He became upset with me and insisted I change into a dress. I desperately did not want to wear a dress to Disneyland and felt that he was being unreasonable. I begged him to let me make this decision myself. No way. He said I couldn't go if I didn't put on a dress. So I stayed home, and he took the boys without me.

I was in bed when Dennis and Danny got home that night. It had been a hard day for me emotionally. Danny ran into my room to see if I was still awake and whispered to me, "Mom, guess who we saw at Disneyland today?"

"Who did you see?"

"We saw Judy and Janelle! And guess what they were wearing?! They were wearing pants! I can't believe Dad tried to make you wear a dress!" Janelle was the pastor's daughter-in-law, and at ten years old Danny was already laughing about his dad's behavior. He was also taking on the role of validating and protecting me. Although I did not intentionally impose my emotional welfare on Danny, because I was so needy of the validation, I gladly accepted this from him.

Years later, I learned that it causes a child emotional pain to have to take responsibility for a parent in such a manner. Danny has since shared with me that he often felt like he was the parent instead of the child. While it was mostly his dad who put him in this role, I regret sometimes leaning on my son emotionally in times of distress when he was in high school and college. I should not have done that. I crossed some boundaries that I didn't even recognize as boundaries at the time.

The truth is my son was the only other person who knew what life was like in our home. With my friends, I was always trying to protect Dennis from being viewed as a jerk. I made excuses for him and denied (even to myself) that I was unhappy, probably more as a coping mechanism than anything else. I was programmed to look on the bright side and rise above my difficulties. My dad would say, "Don't go through life trading one set of problems for another. Accept the problems you have and work on them instead of thinking the grass is greener somewhere else." And that is exactly what I tried to do for twenty-seven years. Danny, unfortunately, became an occasional crutch for me to lean on when I was feeling low.

One of the hardest conversations I ever had to have with my son occurred after he was married. Danny and I got on the subject of his childhood, and he unloaded some of his emotions on me, including the ways *I* had let him down as a parent. He was not trying to hurt me. He was sharing the pain he had felt as a young child living in our dysfunctional home. It was pain he didn't feel that I had fully understood. He insisted that he had never wanted me to stay with his dad. I didn't share his perspective and got defensive. Plus, I still believed I had made the right decision to stay, even though the marriage ultimately ended. I was convinced that it was better for Danny that his parents were together until he left home. I *wanted* to believe I had done the right thing as a mother. So at first I countered some of his conclusions, but in the middle of the conversation, I suddenly realized that his perspective was the only perspective that should matter to me in that moment. It would accomplish nothing to disagree with him or defend myself. My adult child needed to be heard. And I was not going to make the mistake of trying to silence him. So I did my best through tears to listen and validate him.

While Danny shared his pain, I could not help but reflect on a couple of specific occasions when I had informed my dad of his faults as a father. My criticisms were not unjustified, but it was the harsh realization that I too was a flawed person and parent that caused me to feel a flood of compassion for my dad.

I realized all children have some sort of grievance with their parents for how they were raised. No parent is perfect.

I realized that I had said things to my dad that had probably crushed him the way my son's words were unintentionally crushing me, and I determined from that point on to show grace to my dad. He is also a wounded person with holes in his heart, in need of forgiveness. That doesn't mean everything he ever said or did was okay. My dad wouldn't say it was okay either. He has expressed regret and remorse to me for things he would do differently if he could. I believe him and I forgive him.

I asked Danny's forgiveness that day, and even a few times since then. Instead of telling him he is wrong when we don't see eye to eye or he feels the need to revisit certain times in his life, I try to feel his pain. I know we see life differently. Children are not clones of their parents, and I can honestly say that I have never wanted to make Danny my clone. It doesn't bother me for him to have his own opinions that do not reflect mine. We will always be looking at life from different stages of the journey. No mother does everything right, no matter how hard she tries. That includes me. But an emotionally battered wife has a unique set of challenges as a mother, and I have begun to experience freedom from self-condemnation in simply accepting that as a fact of my life.

In hindsight, I believe I did well to do as many things right as I did. I played a critical role when it came to Danny's emotional and relational development. I had a lot to counterbalance when it came to co-parenting with an abusive narcissist, and there were certainly areas where I failed. But with my words and with my actions, I tried to be a positive role model in being long-suffering, loving, and forgiving. I stressed the value of integrity and self-awareness and discouraged hypocrisy as I openly confronted and struggled with challenges in my own life.

I gave Danny my word as he entered his high school years that although I would make mistakes as a parent, I would make those mistakes while trying to do what was right for him individually rather than succumbing to the pressure to uphold rules and regulations I didn't even agree with in our church group. He was my son, and I was accountable to God for parenting him, not every other kid in our church. There was always peer pressure to enforce ridiculous rules collectively, backing up our pastor's authority and making it easier on fellow parents. I didn't agree with this mindset. On the other hand, I felt conflicted about the stand I took. I didn't want to upset friends by allowing Danny to do things forbidden to the others. But ultimately Danny was my priority. And my conviction proved to be one I would never regret.

I have loved my son unconditionally from the day he was born, and I have put my heart into being the best mother I possibly could be. I've instilled what I believe are important values in him. I've never tried to control him or interfere in his life. And I have taken pride in not putting expectations or demands on him or his time.

I know from experience how burdensome it is to have a difficult mother-in-law—the stress that relationship can put on a marriage. So when Danny got married, I made it a high priority to be the kind of mother and mother-in-law who never put demands or expectations on either of them—individually or as a couple. I told Danny long before he was in a serious relationship that when he got married, his first priority should always be his wife, not his mother. I would not expect him to be loyal or defend me if his future wife had a problem with me. I never wanted him to make her feel that she had to please me or have my approval. I even asked him not to brag on my cooking to the woman he might marry. I didn't want her to have any reason to resent me or view me as a rival right off the bat. I was so determined to be the best mother-in-law any bride could ever have!

Keeping with my goal of being "low-maintenance," I have never asked the kids to choose our home for Thanksgiving or Christmas dinner. I have never expected special attention on my birthday. I've never requested them to spend Mother's Day with me. And I don't expect regular phone calls or visits. I'm perfectly happy to talk to them whenever they feel like talking, as opposed to them feeling an obligation to call.

Perhaps I take my "never be a bother" approach to an extreme, after trying to keep a narcissist happy for nearly three decades. I was conditioned to make my needs a low priority for many years. So I certainly won't try to pretend my motivations are all rooted in emotional health, but combined with that obvious baggage is the driving desire to *only enhance* the lives of my "kids," as I call them. And I view giving them plenty of physical and emotional space as my gift to them. I believe that if I'm going to err on one side or the other, it's better to make myself scarce than risk being intrusive. I live by the philosophy that I'd rather have them want to see me and talk to me *more* than wish to see me and talk to me *less*. And I also want to live my own life, not live mine through theirs. That is the healthy part.

You may think I sound like the ideal mother-in-law, but my hands-off approach is because I'm quite performance-driven in relationships and want to meet the expectations of others while keeping *my* needs and expectations to a minimum. Therefore, my "no expectations" policy has formed an identity that helps me feel good about myself.

Well, with that in mind, fast forward to a few months ago and a stressful moment between my son and me. *Hole in her heart Mom* (aka me) was feeling like I might have inserted myself into a situation where I wasn't needed or particularly wanted. In hindsight, this was my paranoia kicking in; my *worst fear on steroids*. I was looking for affirmation that my presence was desired. My imagination took on a life of its own as I sat in the back seat of their family minivan while Danny and Rebecca were talking in the front seats. They were distracted by a problem they were trying to solve (I couldn't hear their conversation from where I was.) The stress they were dealing with did not involve me, but I began to doubt they wanted me there. I started to melt down inside. I offered to take the next flight home because of the intensity of my emotion. If only I could have been relaxed and less fearful. But in those moments, I literally felt desperate to "get out of their way" just as speedily as I could.

When Danny and I got out and tried to talk about it in the heat of the moment, it didn't go well. I felt embarrassed that I might have mistakenly believed they wanted me there, and I was defensive. But I also felt unappreciated because I was there to be helpful, not to intrude. What I needed was really just a hug and assurance that my presence was appreciated. But instead, Danny was short with me. We went back and forth a few times and then Danny said these ten little words that rocked my whole self-image as a mother: "I feel like I have to be perfect for you."

I got mad and walked away from him.

I no longer felt defensive. I was angry. I was overwhelmed with frustration because I *knew* I had not put conditions or expectations on my son. I felt, and may have said, "How can you say that to me?" This is the one thing I believed could *never* be said to me by my son (legitimately). It had been one of my highest priorities as a mother not to do that to him; not to be like Dennis.

I *wanted* to say, "No, you felt that way with your dad and now I'm the only living parent, so you're transferring that onto me. But that's not fair because I have *not* done that to you!" However, I resisted the impulse to go *there* in my anger.

An avalanche of emotion was triggered by his words; a lifetime of frustration—trying so hard to do things right and always falling short, feeling misjudged and misunderstood by the most important people in my life—came over me. I also felt a deep disappointment that perhaps my relationship with Danny wasn't even as good as I thought it was. The pain that welled up inside me was *familiar*. It was the same way I used to feel interacting with Dennis. And that wasn't the first time I'd felt it, but I had never verbalized this to Danny.

Once I calmed down, I told him I was sorry for overreacting and walking away from him, but that I still could not understand how he could feel that way. And he asked me this question: "Mom, do I ever make you feel the way Dad made you feel, even though you know I'm not trying to do that to you?"

I had always been careful not to express that to Danny. I would never have wanted him to think I was comparing him to his dad or trying to be hurtful. But when asked directly, I answered honestly, "Yes, I have felt that way many times." And that was his point.

"Mom, we have the same wounds. You have them as a wife. I have them as a son. But we both project Dad onto each other and react to each other as if we're still interacting with him."

Wow. Talk about throwing the lights on.

In a separate conversation, I once said to Danny, "I have always tried to be a good mother." And he responded, "Why does it always have to be about being good? Can't it be enough that we love each other?"

Filtered through the holes in my heart, I interpreted my son's questions as an evaluation: *I can't honestly say you were a good mother. So it will have to be enough that we love each other.* And I wrestled with his words for months. However, with time and objective reflection, I've reached a different conclusion. I do think he deliberately withheld the validating words I would have preferred to hear in that moment, but not to make me feel like a bad mother. I believe Danny wanted to shatter the performance-driven relationship in favor of a love-driven relationship—for both of us. It's the only way to be free from fear.

Only a love-driven relationship has the power to heal and transform us. That's why Jesus came; to exchange a performance-driven relationship for a love-driven relationship. Because my performance will never be enough, but love never fails.

Chapter 7
CONFLICT

"His goal in verbal conflict is not to negotiate different desires, understand each other's experiences, or think of mutually beneficial solutions. He wants only to win.... Anger and conflict are not the problem; they are normal aspects of life. Abuse doesn't come from people's inability to resolve conflicts but from one person's decision to claim a higher status than another." —Lundy Bancroft

"Conflict is always about an issue. If someone is picking on you or putting you down, you are not experiencing conflict; you are experiencing disrespect and abuse." —Leslie Vernick

A NEW EXTERNAL STRESS BEGAN TO COMPOUND OUR marital struggles in 1992. Our pastor announced that God had told him to move to Tennessee and that everyone in the church was supposed to go with him. God said it. He was the messenger, and following him was following God. He didn't make any allowance for God speaking to individuals or families. If we didn't comply, he said publicly that he feared for our souls. I did not fear that my soul was in jeopardy if I didn't move, but if all my family and closest friends were moving to Tennessee, I couldn't imagine not going. And I couldn't imagine being left behind in California with Dennis.

Dennis resented the pressure being imposed on him by Brother Mears, and he resented me because I argued in favor of going. I never demanded that we move. I never gave any ultimatums, but I did express my desire to go and tried to make persuasive arguments that it was the best decision for Danny—because that's what I believed at the time.

Dennis loved California and had no desire to move to Tennessee, but after we took a trip to the area to look around at the end of 1992, he came to the conclusion that it was probably the thing to do. So we moved in early 1993. However, his resentment and bitterness continued to grow. In many ways, he never stopped blaming and punishing me for the disruption to his life. Any time something went wrong, he would blame it on moving to Tennessee and make a remark about what a mistake it had been to move there *for me*.

He had not been going to church much when the move was announced. If he had been in one of his church phases, he would have accepted anything Brother Mears told us to do with a compliant attitude, rather than expressing his frustration. Since he wasn't in one of those phases, he made sarcastic remarks to certain friends about his life being messed with.

In March of 1993 we moved to Hendersonville, just outside of Nashville, Tennessee. I remember Dennis attending services for a while after we moved. Our church had four two and a half-hour-long services every week. On top of that, we had been urged to move to an area that wasn't close to our temporary church building, so everyone had a long drive to church. And the climate was different, to say the least. Dennis had a lifelong struggle with his weight and comfort was a big issue for him. He did not like to get dressed up, especially in the heat and humidity of summer. In our church, men were expected to wear coats and ties to church. If he gained weight and couldn't wear his "church clothes" comfortably, he just didn't go. That certainly wasn't the only reason he was hot and cold in attendance. But it was a contributing factor.

Dennis was a person of extremes. Hot and cold were his two temperatures in just about everything. He was in either a really good mood or a really bad mood. He could shift between the two on a dime, and when he was in a bad mood he was also combative. I learned to live as though walking on eggshells to avoid setting him off. I wasn't consciously walking on eggshells. I just lived that way like it was my auto-pilot, but my emotional radar was always up. Living this way for so long, I learned what set Dennis off and adapted as much as I could to avoid his unpleasant responses. I felt responsible for Dennis' emotional state. I wound up feeling responsible for everyone's emotions in my life. Whenever there was conflict between friends or family members, I felt like it was my job to fix it. I still do and have had to work hard to overcome this type of codependence.

As predictable as Dennis was, sometimes the things that would set him off were so random and baffling, I could not for the life of me understand his dramatic reactions. He had so much anger simmering inside him all the time, I don't even think he always understood why he reacted the way he did.

During heated phone conversations if someone made him mad, he would not just raise his voice and talk over the other person; he would visibly tremble. I could watch his blood pressure rise. And he had conflict with everyone at some point. Whether it was me, members of his family, members of my family, friends, or business associates, he was unable to deal with conflict in a healthy way. He went off on people. It could rarely, if ever, be kept to a simple disagreement or difference of opinion. If you did not agree that he was right, he would have to prove you wrong or make you pay. There would often be character assassination, insults, bullying, and even threats.

One time he was talking to a contractor in California who was renovating an investment house. He asserted that Dennis owed him more money for additional work and Dennis disagreed. Dennis got louder and louder. I saw his hands shaking, his face getting red, beads of perspiration on his forehead. I thought he was going to have a stroke. He was also vindictive and would find ways to make people pay for their behavior. I listened frequently as he spoke abrasively and condescendingly over the phone to loan processors and underwriters, wondering how they were feeling on the other end of the line. When he was working on a loan and clients were difficult to deal with, he'd hang up the phone and say to himself, "Your points just went up, my friend." There were numerous times he chased someone in his car to intimidate them if he got cut off in traffic or someone flipped him off. He especially loved to get out of the vehicle to intimidate them with his size.

When Danny was around ten years old, we drove a motor home to San Francisco for a vacation. I don't even remember what set him off, but Dennis had one of his violent episodes of road rage toward another driver. In *his* mind, he was defending his family's safety. He got out of the motor home at a red light and went up to the window of the other driver, insisting that he "be a man" and get out of his vehicle. Danny and I were scared and felt anything but safe as we watched Dennis yell at a complete stranger in a busy intersection full of traffic. There was an incident in a Santa Barbara grocery store when a cashier touched Danny to move him out of the way and Dennis became irate. He went off on the guy and rudely told him never to put his hand on someone else's kid. I watched the whole thing. The guy obviously meant no harm and tried to explain he was just nudging Danny out of the way to get around him. Dennis got louder, telling him even more emphatically, "I don't think you understood me. There is no reason *whatsoever* for you to put your hands on my kid." I was mortified and tried to convey my apologies through eye contact because I dared not say a word.

Not long after my mom died, my youngest brother, Chris, moved in with us for a short time. He was seventeen, and he and my dad were not getting along. They were dealing with the pain of losing Mom in their own ways and were clashing. One day Chris picked Danny up from school for us and Danny confessed to his dad that Chris had taken him to Music Plus after picking him up and had played an AC/DC cassette in the car. Danny was not allowed to go in music stores without his dad. This might have been a reasonable boundary for a ten-year-old, but it was rooted in fear and rumination-control. Dennis viewed all heavy metal as satanic, and Danny was forbidden to listen to any kind of rock music. This was late 1987 or early 1988. Danny was no more than ten years old, and at that age he usually confessed if he had been exposed to anything forbidden. Danny told his dad he had asked Chris not to play the music with him in the car, but Chris played it anyway. When Dennis found out, he blew up and confronted Chris in a very threatening way. He didn't hit him, but he grabbed him by the shirt, shoved him against the wall, and held him there in an act of intimidation. Chris was five years old when I married Dennis, so he'd had plenty of experience with his temper. He acknowledged what he'd done and apologized. Then he made himself scarce until Dennis cooled off.

One time in 1990 we were at my aunt and uncle's house with other extended family. We were sitting around the kitchen table playing cards. Danny was twelve years old and was walking around behind everyone, viewing their cards. Clearly, it was making some of the card players uncomfortable. Danny then made an innocent comment, which resulted in my uncle cautioning Danny not to cheat. It wasn't an accusation. My uncle even said it with a laugh, but what had been a friendly family gathering turned extremely awkward and uncomfortable in an instant as Dennis stood up ferociously and threw his hand down in a disgusting rant. It was so embarrassing. *Why do you have to act this way?* I would think to myself every time one of these situations would happen.

Around this same time Danny, at his young age, would protect others from his dad's lack of self-control. He would allow kids smaller than himself to harass him and hit him without fighting back. I always thought Danny was just passive, but years later he told me the real reason he never defended himself. He knew that if a fight broke out and his dad thought the other child was picking on him, his dad would lose it. He didn't want that to happen and felt like it was his responsibility to prevent the conflict by silently accepting antagonism and even punches. He actually hoped, in those moments, that his dad didn't notice what was going on.

Dennis had an explosive temper, especially when he thought someone was harming his son (even if there was no harm being done). He would say it was about protecting Danny, but it wasn't about Danny at all. If his motivation had been purely Danny's welfare, he would have seen what his outbursts did to Danny emotionally and protected Danny from himself. Instead the perceived offenses against Danny were personal violations to Dennis. If Danny had tried to talk to his dad about his feelings, Dennis would have rejected the idea that he was inflicting emotional injury on Danny. Dennis really had no idea how his behavior affected others nor did he see anything wrong with his blowups.

Within months of the card-playing incident, friends of ours had come over to discuss the details of a business investment that had become complicated. These were good friends. We had traveled together. Our kids were close friends. Danny and one of their sons were playing in Danny's room as the four of us sat in the dining room discussing business. Dennis and the husband were disagreeing about certain details of the joint business venture. Our friend suggested something to which Dennis took offense. He thought he was being accused of dishonesty. In the blink of an eye, he was going off on our friend, verbally assaulting him. Our friend made the mistake of pointing at Dennis while explaining that a certain task had been Dennis' responsibility. He did not put his finger in Dennis' face. He just pointed in his direction. Dennis went ballistic, threatening, "I'll break that finger off and feed it to you if you don't get it out of my face!" I wanted to crawl under the table. The boys were at the other end of the house, but they heard it all. They remain close friends today and can look back and laugh about that night, but at the time, the confrontation was scary to them.

One would imagine that Dennis would have been embarrassed by his behavior, but he rarely was. He bragged about that confrontation and the way he had put our friend in his place. He occasionally retold the story and got a big laugh out of it. Dennis alienated many friends over the years. There were a number of times that he invited someone to move in with us to help them through a transition or a difficult time in their life. It never ended well. In every situation I can recall, it started and ended the same way. He would generously extend an open-ended invitation, telling the friend to feel at home and help themselves to anything in the kitchen. He always started out being such a great guy. The friends were always appreciative and took him up on the hospitality. Then it would be no time at all before every little thing they did irritated him. He would start picking them apart to me in private. He resented them being in his chair, monopolizing his television, or using too much hot water. He would complain to me if they were stretched out on the couch and didn't show him respect by making room for him in his regular spot when he entered the room. He resented them eating our food or not offering theirs. He resented their personal habits and would complain that they were lazy. If he had only set some boundaries up front and communicated in a healthy way, the situations could have been resolved so differently. But he was not capable of that. In every situation, he felt exploited and victimized almost immediately. In every situation, he felt wronged. He had two modes; hero and martyr. He never felt like anybody appreciated anything he did, which was simply not true. How his rage would be triggered varied, but ultimately the explosion would come.

When Dennis exploded it was usually pretty ugly. He would unload every pent up frustration in one conversation. There was nothing anyone could say to appease him when he was angry. There was no such thing as the right words or the right response. Once his wrath was triggered, someone had to pay. Most of the time it was me. But plenty of others experienced his wrath at least once. One day in late 1990 Dennis went to my brother's house to set him straight about something his wife had said to Danny. Dennis handled the situation horribly. As I sat in the car praying, he confronted Todd on the front porch. I heard Dennis raise his voice. He must not have liked the way my brother responded because he shoved Todd hard. My brother wasn't as big as Dennis, but he certainly isn't a small guy either. He was a successful wrestler in high school, and I'm sure he could defend himself in a fight. But he was caught completely off guard, and he fell down into the flower bed. I was appalled. I hated the behavior, and I hated that I had to go home with this bully. I cried on the ride home.

Many years after this event, it was shared with me by another family member that Todd had not understood why I didn't get out of the car or challenge Dennis' behavior that day. It gave the impression that I supported him in his tirade. I was shocked by that. I never imagined that my silence would be construed as supportive. I just assumed anybody would realize that I lived with this kind of intimidation and explosive anger to an even greater degree at home and didn't have the option to challenge him in front of other people. But my former sister-in-law and I spent some time together last spring and she said something that put this in perspective for me. As a member of Dennis' family, she said they always perceived me as united with Dennis in his words and actions. They viewed us as a team. She didn't see me as someone being oppressed by his domination. She said, "You backed him up, defended him when there was other family conflict. You seemed to think he was great." Her perception of our relationship was enlightening for me.

She also had no idea he used me as a mouthpiece more than once when he wanted to convey negative feelings to his brother. Little did she (or Dennis' brother) know that Dennis had dictated *his* feelings to me more than once, coaching me on how to write an email expressing *our* feelings to his brother. They regularly had periods of estrangement and didn't speak for months at a time. Dennis would say he never wanted anything to do with his brother again and bash him to me. I'm not asserting that I never felt hurt by my brother-in-law or that none of the feelings I expressed in communication with him were genuinely mine. But I always urged Dennis to work things out and be on good terms. Family has always been important to me and I wanted a good relationship with my in-laws, as well as my own family. When Dennis did patch things up with his brother, I asked if he would please take ownership of the statements (in emails I had written) that were really coming from him rather than letting me take the fall. But he refused. One time we had borrowed money from his brother to get us through a difficult cash flow period. Once the crisis passed and we had plenty of money coming in again, I voiced my conviction that Dan should be paid back before we spent money on any luxuries or nonessentials. Dennis flatly disagreed and told me not to tell him what to do. He said he would pay Dan back gradually and that Dan didn't need the money. I felt badly about taking our time when we were able to pay the money back much more promptly. It genuinely bothered my conscience. But I had no say in those decisions. Of course, Dan didn't know that I was trying to look out for him behind closed doors and I'm not sure he'd even believe me if I told him. But it's the truth.

When my former sister-in-law shared her perception of me as always being "on the same team" with him, a light was turned on concerning my own family. If Dennis' family had perceived me this way, of course my family must have as well! I did defend Dennis and back him up. I did always try to put him in the best light. But this wasn't because I was necessarily in agreement with him. My role was the buffer between him and other people. It was a learned behavior. It was the only way I knew how to survive. It was the only option I believed I had. And I also loved Dennis. I was trying with all my might to have a good marriage with a raging bully who was regularly abusive toward me.

The outbursts that others experienced, as bad as they were, didn't compare with the outbursts I experienced in private. So his public temper, though often embarrassing, wasn't my biggest challenge. A second cousin told me years after the card game incident that her parents had always felt so sorry for me. If Dennis blew up like that in front of a group of people, they could only imagine what my home life must be like. I was grateful for their insight. It meant a lot to me to know they *realized* (without my telling them) that I wasn't in agreement with his behavior. My friend Janette begged me not to stay with Dennis after a violent episode in 1999. She was outspoken and had occasionally clashed with Dennis. She thought I was in denial of the kind of marriage I was in, since I always defended Dennis to her. It wasn't outright denial. That's just what battered women do.

After I filed for divorce in 2002, I was flooded with validating comments from people who had never told me what they really thought (as long as I was determined to stay in the marriage). I was surprised by how many people actually did see through my upbeat exterior and recognized I was suffering abuse severe enough to justify leaving despite the legalistic climate of the church. I feared being judged because, in our church, the person who left and filed for divorce was always considered the one at fault. I was surprised because, while I expected support from my closest friends, I expected judgment from others.

One friend who never clashed with Dennis and loved him very much dared to tell me that she and her husband feared I might eventually be the victim of a murder/suicide. She risked my being offended or sharing the concern with Dennis because my life was more important to her than her comfort. I will never forget that. The same friend also stood up for me when she accidentally dialed his number after we were separated. He went on the attack, accusing her of taking sides, saying that he thought she was *his friend too* and not just mine. She did not back down. She told him the truth about how much she disliked the way he treated me, and even though she loved him, she couldn't be neutral for that reason. She would never have sought out that conversation, but she didn't shrink back when he started in on her. When she told me what she'd said to him, I was more than grateful. I was stunned. I was so accustomed to everyone backing away from Dennis just to avoid having to deal with him. I wasn't used to anybody sticking up for me.

Occasionally I'd hear of someone saying, "Shari is the only person I know who could have lived with Dennis that long." That always validated me, but after my separation I was shocked to hear how many people actually feared for my life. Several friends admitted to me that they worried Dennis might possibly kill me one day; then kill himself following a blind rage. I had no idea anybody had those kinds of concerns for me, other than the one friend. I wondered why nobody told me they were concerned for my safety when I was with him. They probably believed that I would tell them it could never happen. And that is probably exactly how I would have responded, but I still think they should have been honest with me.

People always tried to stay out of Dennis' way. For me, staying out of his way was impossible. Most of the time, I felt quite alone in my corner of the ring.

Chapter 8
FEAR

"Certain mental illnesses can increase the chance that an abuser will be dangerous and use physical violence. . . . Even if the mental illness is properly treated, his abusiveness won't necessarily change." —Lundy Bancroft

IN NOVEMBER 1994, DENNIS' THIRTY-ONE-YEAR-OLD sister died suddenly from pneumonia. She was young and healthy. Her pneumonia was initially misdiagnosed as a pulled muscle. While she rested on her sofa waiting for test results, she died tragically and prematurely of a treatable condition. In November 1997, Dennis' mother died following a stroke at the age of seventy. The stroke also came suddenly during a visit with family in Cincinnati. Since their father had died of electrocution around the age of forty-six, Dennis and his brother were now the only ones remaining in their immediate family.

The deaths of Dennis' sister and mother were hard losses for him. When his mother's life was still hanging in the balance, he started to fight a battle with overwhelming guilt for the way he had been living his life. He seemed to believe that if he could make things right with every person he had wronged, maybe God would heal her. His depression and irrational spiritual fears, I'm convinced, were rooted in the unhealthy warnings his mother gave him about the consequences for his actions (like when his mother told him that their house burned down because the family had played cards the night before). Rather than teaching him that bad things happen to everyone because we live in a broken world, she taught him that bad things happened because people angered God. Brother Mears reinforced Dennis' fears and phobias by frequently saying that mental institutions were full of people with guilty consciences whose real problem was sin.

Fear and avoidance were as deeply ingrained in Dennis as *facing* my fears and getting them behind me was ingrained in me. I could never relate to his phobias, but I was sensitive to them for his sake. When his mother died Dennis began to sink deeper and deeper into a black hole. He seemed to feel responsible in some way for her death. The waxing and waning depression Dennis battled went into a deeper psychosis. For two full years, there was frequent talk of suicide on his part. This marked the beginning of the two most agonizing years of my whole life.

Dennis was not just depressed. He became psychotic. He had typical signs of depression and anxiety, such as panic attacks and not wanting to get out of bed some days. But he also exhibited more extreme symptoms of psychosis. He cried a lot, broke into cold sweats, suffered from tremors, and ruminated constantly on his fears and phobias. He also hinted at the possibility of suicide on a regular basis. It broke my heart to witness him so wracked with fear. Of course, the guilt, fear and depression catapulted him back into church attendance and compulsive rule-following in order to make his world feel safer. But his rule-following was centered on Danny and me. Although he still lived at home, Danny was an adult in college during all of this, not a little kid. Dennis questioned both of us continually about where we were going and what we were doing, what we were watching on television, what we were reading in magazines. I was asked not to wear pants, not to wear earrings, not to go to the movies. By late 1998, I was going to counseling with Dennis regularly and on my own occasionally. I learned that I absolutely had to stand up to his demands. I tried to reason with him and told him that I didn't think any of those things were wrong, and he pleaded with me to just do what he asked of me for him and his peace of mind. At the root of his controlling behavior was his desperation to escape the ruminations. He was attempting to control his thoughts, fears, and anxiety by controlling us. When boiled down to the motive behind the madness, it did not have anything to do with God. It was all about Dennis not wanting to worry and ruminate. If he could keep us from doing anything that worried him, he thought he could have peace of mind. But he never had peace and neither did we.

Dennis was controlling and would make sure that we wouldn't watch anything that would trigger his worries about angering God. Danny was continually asked not to watch Swami on ESPN because of the connection between predictions and fortune telling. He would pay close attention to promos for upcoming talk show topics and if any kind of psychic or someone who made predictions was an upcoming guest, he would make a point of asking us to promise we would not watch the show. He knew we didn't believe in mediums or psychics, but it wasn't about what we believed. He feared us even watching a show the same day such a guest made an appearance. If we did, he would ruminate about it. Suddenly, Dennis (always a David Letterman fan) didn't think we should be watching shows like Letterman because the content might be displeasing to God. He didn't want me to go to a Vince Gill concert because Budweiser was one of the sponsors. He tried to manipulate me by asking condescendingly, "Doesn't it bother your conscience at all?" But the same person who was trying to be the spiritual leader was often curled up in a fetal position in our bed in the middle of the day. He would often request that I huddle there with him, which was agonizing for me whether I said yes or no. I would offer to pray with him instead.

One night, before the concert, I told him I didn't appreciate his trying to be my conscience and suggesting I was spiritually inferior to him just because it didn't bother me to go to a concert sponsored by Budweiser. I told him I felt like he was manipulating me. "I don't want to hurt your feelings," I said. "But I cannot be led spiritually by someone who is making all their decisions out of irrational fear. It isn't healthy for me to go along with you in these unreasonable demands. I am going to the concert." Once he realized he wasn't going to deter me, he changed his mind and went with me to the concert. His behavior was just bizarre.

The pressure to comply with his demands was intense. But it wasn't the healthy conscience of a man trying to lead his family spiritually. It wasn't even leadership. It was twisted, self-serving manipulation cloaked in spiritual concern. Here was a person consumed with shame, guilt, and fear attempting to impose shame, guilt, and fear on Danny and me almost continuously. It was emotional torture. He even went to Brother Mears and reported on his own son.

Danny was planning to go to a baseball game (something Brother Mears regarded as worldly and strongly discouraged) during a trip to California to visit friends. Dennis had not been able to talk him out of both the baseball game and wearing shorts. So Dennis took it to Brother Mears, thinking Brother Mears might be able to convince him. Brother Mears did try to persuade Danny to change his plans, but Danny made no promises to him. That was how Danny found out his dad had attempted to control him by talking to Brother Mears about him. Dennis was afraid that if Danny broke the rules he might be susceptible to an evil spirit. I realized my husband was seriously mentally ill at this point. I was so thankful that Danny had a life outside our home. He could escape the madness and have some sense of normalcy.

My life during these two years was sheer hell. I was determined to be a good wife. I put myself on the back burner (if I even had a burner) and devoted myself to being the rock my husband needed me to be. I hoped that if I could just hang in there with him through this ordeal, perhaps he would eventually emerge from it, life would go on, and I would have his undying gratitude. He would finally appreciate me. I would never have to jump through another hoop to prove my love and devotion. My character would never be assassinated again. I would have proven my love in such a convincing way that it would never be in question. I tried to view it as an opportunity, an investment in my future. This type of sacrifice came naturally because my whole life had revolved around proving myself to God and other people from the day I was born.

During those two years, Dennis had many appointments with medical doctors, psychiatrists, psychotherapists, and Christian counselors. Dennis begged me to go with him. He said, "You articulate what is happening to me better than I do. It's such a big help to have you there. I need you. Please don't make me go alone." And so I went with him to every appointment to give moral support and speak for him. I was the interpreter who explained to the professionals all the elements of his condition that I've explained in this book. It was tiring, but I do believe I was able to clarify the spiritual aspect of his depression in a way they might have struggled to grasp in my absence. After all, I had been watching these fears and phobias manifest at differing intensities for twenty-two years.

There were peaks and valleys throughout this two-year ordeal. Dennis tried a wide variety of drugs, including anti-psychotics to lessen the ruminations. He was taking a heavy dose of anti-anxiety medication throughout the day. And he was, of course, taking a high dose of anti-depressant. All of these drugs had various side effects, but they were necessary. He could not function without them. The professionals even suggested electro-shock therapy, which Dennis declined.

Dennis talked about killing himself a lot. He would usually say it in an apologetic way, telling me that he just couldn't keep doing this to Danny and me. If he killed himself, the torture would end for all of us. Even when I knew I was being manipulated, I had to convince him that suicide was not the answer, that Danny and I did not want it to end that way. I didn't want to take that chance. One never knows.

At one point the professionals urged me to have Dennis committed. Dennis had always feared being in a mental ward. It was one of his worst fears, and I could not put him there. I will never forget a specific phone call. During this time, we were primarily living on the income from his real estate investments. He wanted to get away from making so many trips back and forth to California and having so much time on his hands when he was in Tennessee. He decided that being busier might help his condition, so he'd taken a job at a mortgage company as a loan officer. During his good days he could function well enough without coworkers being aware of the shape he was in. During a bad day, if he felt an anxiety attack coming on, he would pop a Klonopin and get some relief. One day he called and told me that he wanted to go to the roof and jump. I talked him out of it but then immediately called his psychiatrist's office. The nurse said Dennis needed to be hospitalized immediately. I told her he would never agree to that. She said that as his wife I could make the decision for him, and I would have their support. All I had to do was say the word and they would have picked him up. I told her I just could not do that to him, and she responded abruptly, "If you won't take my advice, then there's nothing I can do to help you." At the time, I thought she was cold. But now I understand the position I was putting her in. I was refusing her professional advice.

During those two years Dennis continually told me he didn't know of another woman who wouldn't have left him. He couldn't believe I was still there. He frequently thanked me for standing by him, and he depended on me like a baby depends on its mother. At one point I decided to get an office job to help out financially. Dennis thought it was a good idea because our finances were suffering. I also just wanted to get out of the house. I wasn't making a lot of money and it wasn't a job I enjoyed, but it was a distraction. It was better than being tethered to him. I don't remember how long it lasted. I just remember Dennis begging me to quit within weeks. He said he'd thought he wanted me to go to work, but actually he needed me to be available at all times. If I was working in an office, I could not be on the other end of the phone whenever he needed to talk. Like every other time he'd asked me to quit a job, I asked him to promise me that he wasn't going to again belittle me for not contributing financially. I begged him to be absolutely sure he wanted me to quit my job. (This issue was ongoing throughout our entire marriage. He wanted me to work; then he didn't want me to work.) He promised he would never suggest I get a job again. He definitely wanted me to quit. So I quit.

In May 1999 I turned forty. Friends threw a party for me. They came out to the car to get me with a walker and escorted me to the front door. They put a crown on my head and a scepter in my hand, proclaiming me queen. It was a fun night. I wore my crown the entire evening. And I took both the crown and scepter home, along with my gifts, as souvenirs of the occasion. I had no idea that Dennis was ruminating about the scepter. It looked too much like a magic wand to him. He asked me to throw the scepter away so he wouldn't worry about it. By this time, I had been living with these irrational fears and demands for a year and a half. His fears were controlling him and he was in turn attempting to control me with his fears. My greatest fear was that this would never end if I continued to humor and enable him. And I was reaching the end of my rope. I knew I could not live this way much longer. I was growing so weary of these conversations. It felt like things were only getting worse, and I began to more strongly resist his demands. It was a breaking point for me.

Dennis had the scepter in his hand and was pressing me hard to let him throw it away. It wasn't about the scepter. I have no idea where it is today. It was what the request represented. He was demanding that I give up any control over my own life and choices in order to appease him and calm his irrational fears. It was wrong and unhealthy to comply. I had been complying for a year and a half, and he was in a worse condition than ever. I clearly wasn't helping him by always giving in. I refused to let him throw it away, but he wouldn't take no for an answer. He was desperate to take that scepter out of my hands and in my own desperation, I drew a line here. Ultimately I started crying and yelling at him, "You have pushed me too far! It is *my* scepter from *my* birthday party, and you have no right to tell me I can't have it as a keepsake!" I allowed myself to release a year and a half of frustration in that moment. I remember saying over and over, "I can't do this anymore! I can't do this anymore!" He backed off and never brought it up again. He just moved on to something different.

A month later an old friend was coming to visit me and Dennis decided to go see his brother in California while she was visiting. I was really looking forward to the time apart. Then just before he was going to leave, he started ruminating on the possibility that I might go to a movie with her. He would be gone and wouldn't know (couldn't control) what I was doing. He asked me to promise him that I wouldn't go see a movie. I said I had no plans to go to the movies, but I wasn't going to promise I wouldn't. That triggered panic. He started to cry and shake and beg me to promise, but I held my ground. I remember losing it on this occasion too. I wound up yelling "No! This is not healthy, and I am not going to promise you I won't go! I'm not your child! You should appreciate the fact that I am not willing to do as I please and then lie to you." I didn't know how much longer I could go on this way.

One of my coping strategies was to write to a few close friends about some of the difficult moments. One of the friends I wrote to most when I needed support and encouragement was the same friend who told me her fears for my safety. I knew she loved Dennis and recognized the gravity of my situation better than any of my other friends. Her husband had worked in the psychiatric field for many years and knew my circumstances were volatile and potentially dangerous. There was no way to know for sure if I was sitting on a ticking time bomb about to explode.

By early September 1999 I was feeling deep despair and hopelessness. One Saturday morning I told Dennis that I just needed to get out by myself for the day. I drove to a local mall and walked aimlessly for hours. When I got tired of doing that, I decided to go see a movie. After the movie I headed for home. I remember crying and telling God that I didn't think I could go another step of this journey. I was at the end of my rope and barely hanging on. And then I pleaded, "Please, You have to make a way for my escape. I can't take anymore. I just want out. I don't care how."

When I arrived home it was dark and Dennis was relieved to see me. He wanted to go to Sonic and get something to eat. I told him I wasn't hungry, but he asked if I would ride with him anyway. I agreed. On the ride to the drive-in restaurant, he talked about himself and how he couldn't keep doing this to Danny and me. He said, "I just feel like I should get in the car and start driving and never come back." Of course, I knew this was my cue to reassure him that wasn't what Danny or I wanted. His speech wasn't about me or what any of this was doing to me. It was about him seeking reassurance from me, and I just didn't have the energy to play my role. Instead of responding, I was silent. What he didn't know was that I was silently praying, "Oh, God, please let him mean it and do it. Please let him drive away and never come back." The silence was unbearable for Dennis. He kept talking.

When we got back home and were walking up to the front porch, he tried to make me feel guilty for being so quiet. I made the mistake of telling him honestly how I felt. "You know, I don't think you realize how hard this has been on me and how emotionally drained I am." That was unacceptable.

He went from needy to angry in a flash. He threatened suicide again, not to spare me or Danny any more suffering but to punish me for mentioning that I was having a hard time with my role as caregiver. "Well, I'll just go down to the basement, get my gun, and blow my brains out then!" he spewed venomously, as if that would be his revenge. I almost could not believe my ears. This same person who had said over and over that he didn't know of another woman who would have still been by his side was now threatening to punish me for simply saying I was having a rough day.

I didn't feel a drop of compassion for him at that moment. I felt used and abused. And my response was uncharacteristically angry. I shot back, "F*** you!" And he slapped me hard across the face.

I ran to my van and drove to my brother Chris's house. I knew Danny was there watching a football game, and I called to alert him to what had just happened. I was scared and crying. He told me he was going to call the police. He said he did not want to be the one to find his dad dead or try to talk sense into him if it was more manipulation. He said it was a job for the police. When I got to Chris and Cheryl's house, Danny immediately came out on the front porch and just held onto me, trying to comfort me. I said, "If he did it, it's my fault."

Danny replied, "Mom, if he did it, *it's over*. It's not your fault."

Danny and a friend had been watching the game with my brothers and my dad. When I showed up Todd and my dad quietly left through the garage. They did not come out to the porch to say anything to me and I assumed they didn't want to be involved in the chaos. But Chris, Cheryl, and Danny—who were all very supportive—did try to comfort me. I was still standing on the front porch when a police officer arrived. Danny had told them over the phone that his dad hit me, and the officer urged me to press charges. I refused. I made excuses for Dennis. I said, "You don't understand. He would never really harm me. He's been in a bad depression for almost two years, and I don't want to make things worse. It'll be okay." I could see the frustration in the officer's eyes as he handed me information on domestic abuse and told me he could not protect me if I refused to cooperate, but if I changed my mind to give them a call.

When the officer left, I looked at Cheryl and said, "Tell me the truth. I sounded like a typical battered woman, didn't I?" She nodded, "I'm not going to lie to you. That's exactly what you sounded like."

Dennis did not attempt suicide. He did go to the basement and get one of his guns. But he only drove around town calling friends to say he *wanted* to kill himself. It felt like an episode of *Cops*. One friend convinced Dennis to come to his house and give him the gun. Then the wife of this friend got scared and called me to ask if I thought I should come over there and try to talk to him. I said there was no way I was going anywhere near him. I was sorry Dennis was on his way to their house, but I wasn't the one who involved them. Not long after he had gone there and given the gun to our friend, Dennis called me to say he was sorry for hitting me. And then he tried his best to convince me to come home.

I told him I was not coming home, and I wanted him to stay away to give me some time to pack a bag. I wasn't saying I would never come back. I didn't know what I was going to do. I just needed time to think. He said, "Shari, you know you don't have to be afraid to come home. You know I am not capable of really hurting you."

"Dennis, just five minutes before you hit me in the face, you would have said you weren't capable of *that*," I replied. "I can't know what you are capable of because *you* don't even know what you're capable of. I forgive you, but I *am* afraid of you." For the next six weeks I divided my time between the homes of two close friends. More than one friend suggested I should have asked *him* to leave rather than displacing myself.

However, despite these circumstances, I was still more comfortable displacing myself than Dennis.

We had been going to a Christian counselor named Floyd Dawson. I called the next day for an appointment and told Floyd everything that happened that night. He told me I did the right thing to leave immediately when Dennis threatened suicide (rather than trying to talk him out of it). Dennis had been his patient and he wasn't basing any of his opinions strictly on my version of events. He said that he did not believe Dennis would ever premeditatedly harm or kill me. But in a moment of rage, Floyd assumed he was capable of doing both. He explained that suicide is irrational and so is homicide. A person who is capable of harming themselves is also capable, in that moment, of harming the person closest to them. He said if Dennis had aimed the gun at me and shot me, he probably would have felt immediate remorse and would have to then turn the gun on himself. But I would still be dead. Trying to reason with an irrational person is futile. And Floyd told me he was proud of me for not staying and trying to reason with Dennis. But now I had to figure out what was next. After Dennis hit me in anger that night, I had new concerns for my own safety. His behavior had devastated the one hope I had clung to; that he would appreciate all I had willingly gone through to stand by him. By then I realized there was no hope of receiving respect or gratitude from a narcissist. *His depression didn't cause the abuse. It just magnified it.*

Dennis' psychiatrist said that one of the challenges in treating a person with both depression and anxiety is trying to figure out whether the anxiety is causing the depression or the depression is causing the anxiety. With Dennis it was hard to say. He had many fears. He feared going into a deep depression, which would indicate that the anxiety caused the depression.

But other times, when he wasn't consumed with irrational fears, depression would set in without a trigger, indicating that the depression caused the anxiety. It was probably some of both. The depression that began in 1997 and continued for two full years was deeply rooted in fear. And it was different from any previous depression I had been through with him. My worst fear was that he had suffered a mental break from which he might never recover.

Chapter 9
YOU ARE THE TABLE

"Verbal abuse is a form of emotional maltreatment in which words are systematically used to belittle, undermine, scapegoat, or maliciously manipulate another person. Verbal abuse can be every bit as damaging as physical or sexual abuse, and in some cases it's even more damaging. Those who haven't experienced abuse often can't understand this." —*Steven R. Tracy*

FOR APPROXIMATELY SIX WEEKS IN THE FALL OF 1999 I stayed with close friends. I could have asked Dennis to leave, but I didn't. I thought it would make more sense for me to be the displaced one. After all, Dennis was the one paying the bills, so, in my mind, he should have the house. During that time I tried to figure out if I wanted to end the marriage or reconcile. Dennis was pursuing reconciliation with all his might, but part of me really wanted out. I needed the approval of others to leave, and I thought perhaps fewer people would fault me for not going back to him after the physical abuse. This time, I did not try to keep the violence a secret. I knew it had been a serious mistake to cover for him in the past.

I continued going to counseling during the separation, and Dennis went separately. I told Floyd I wasn't sure what I wanted. He suggested I write down all the ways I felt neglected and abused, and then all the things that would need to change for me to consider returning to the marriage. I worked on the assignment at my friend's house. Janette was one of my closest friends and knew a lot about my ongoing abuse. She was sitting in the same room with me while I typed away. I shared with her what I was working on, and she just shook her head, asking why in the world I would ever consider going back to him.

I was brutally honest in the assignment. I wrote fourteen pages, giving specific examples of degrading and abusive behavior. When Floyd read my thesis he suggested a joint session in which I could read to Dennis what I had written. I was nervous when I arrived at the counseling session. I had a lot of fear and anxiety. I had not been in Dennis' presence since the night he hit me about two weeks earlier. I trembled as I read the examples, waiting for his reaction. I believed Dennis would get mad and reject it completely. After all, he had hit me because I mentioned that I was having a hard time. I thought he might accuse me of lying and verbally attack me (the way he always did in private). But his reaction shocked me.

When I finished reading, he looked contrite. He nodded his head in agreement and said, "Every word is true." And then he went further, tagging it all as typical behavior. This response caught me totally off guard. He repented, asked forgiveness, and promised that if I would consider coming home, he would keep those fourteen pages forever and reread them often to remind him of the patterns of behavior he wanted to break. I will never know if these were moments of sincere remorse and repentance, or just a change in his strategy to manipulate my emotions. But at that time, I believed him to be sincere.

He had started working out and losing weight after I left, taking proactive steps to improve his physical and mental health. During the separation, he seemed to have a miraculous recovery from depression. Suddenly he was able to do all the things he'd claimed he was unable to do for the past two years. And one day, completely out of the blue, he confessed that he had *consciously* manipulated me with his depression. He wasn't saying that he had faked the depression. He was acknowledging that he *used* his depression to control me. He had known what he was doing. A lot of it was calculated. He promised he would never do that to me again. If this was a premeditated tactic to reel me back in by giving me a legitimate reason to trust him, it worked like a charm.

Our twenty-fourth anniversary was October 22, 1999, and I reasoned that the start of our twenty-fifth year would be a new beginning. I gave Dennis a lot of credit for his honesty and humility, and I agreed to come home. I reasoned that his blatant honesty surely was a positive sign. I wanted to believe he could and would change. My goal had never been to get out of the marriage. I was as determined as ever to make it work. So we went to Gatlinburg for our anniversary, vowing to make a fresh start.

The change did not last long at all.

I had mistakenly believed that when the depression ended, my husband might finally appreciate me after the way I stood by him throughout the crisis, but it actually got worse instead of better. There was a honeymoon phase, of course. During those initial months, Dennis dropped a lot of weight and landed a lucrative job as an account executive with a mortgage corporation that made loans to questionable borrowers. (The corporation eventually went out of business and that type of lending became widely known as predatory lending.) He knew financing, especially creative financing, and he did extremely well in that position. He looked great, was making a lot of money, and was feeling successful again. Danny had just graduated from college in May of 2000, and toward the end of the summer, I expressed an interest in returning to school. Dennis encouraged me and told me he was proud of me for wanting to get my degree.

In the fall of 2000 I enrolled at Volunteer State Community College. Before the second semester, though, it became obvious that Dennis had expected me to fail or quit. He became increasingly annoyed when I began to excel. He told me he wasn't interested in hearing about what I was learning. It bored him, he said. He complained that school was becoming my life, but that wasn't the real issue. I made sure I did not neglect my family or any of my responsibilities at home. I took twelve hours or less per semester. The real problem he had was that he resented my *love* of school and the confidence it gave me. He made it difficult for me at times, but I was determined not to be robbed of this opportunity. Plus, I knew that if I let him talk me into quitting college the way he'd talked me into quitting high school, I would have to endure even more dropout jokes for the rest of my life. I was not about to let that happen.

The abuse that came after the major depression was harder to take because I had put so much stock in his changing for the better, but I was not some submissive little lamb who never spoke up for herself. I am a very expressive person, and I tried many times to stand up for myself. I was frequently defending and explaining myself and trying to reason with him. He dominated me verbally, so I would write letters to him instead of trying to have conversations because that was the only way to fully express myself without having my words twisted and used against me. His strategy in any argument was to change the subject by putting me in a defensive position. He always talked over me; he would never let me finish my thoughts.

One afternoon Dennis was telling me some of my faults. I was trying to be open to his criticism rather than be defensive. Because of the counseling I had received, I learned to acknowledge my flaws and was willing to work on them. As he spoke, I nodded in agreement several times to let him know that he was being heard and validated. Several times I said, "You're right. I agree. I do that. I'm sorry." I thought I was doing everything right, and I was so sincere. But suddenly rage flashed in his eyes and he yelled at me, "Stop nodding your head and agreeing! Don't patronize me that way!" I couldn't believe it. There was nothing I could do to please him. I felt sickened by him.

In a calm voice, I said, "Can we please take a break and come back to this after we've both had a chance to cool off a little bit?" He said we needed to finish the conversation right then. I told him I *couldn't* talk anymore (which was unusual for me). He demanded to know why. I told him that it was because of the way I was feeling at that moment, that I was afraid I was going to say something I would regret, and it would be better to stop talking. He demanded to know what I meant by "the way I was feeling." I told him "You don't want to know," and then pleaded with him, "Please, just let it go." He would not. He pressed me hard for an answer and so I reluctantly but honestly said, "I need to stop talking because your reaction is repulsive to me, and I'm tempted to say things I will regret later."

"Oh, so you find me repulsive, huh? I think that's something I probably need to know. I'm so sorry I repulse you." He had succeeded once again in changing the subject and dodging the real issues. I began to apologize for my choice of words. I explained that I didn't find *him* repulsive. I found his *behavior* repulsive. I told him that I didn't mean to hurt him and didn't want to say it, but he insisted. He didn't speak to me again for I don't remember how long.

I saw Floyd the next day and told him everything that happened, expecting him to confirm that I had really screwed up by using the word *repulsive*. Instead, he asked, "Why did you apologize? You were just being honest. You absolutely did the right thing to tell him how you felt about his behavior. You had nothing to apologize for. You just allowed him to manipulate you into believing you were the one in the wrong again." Floyd showed me that I was actually conditioning Dennis to treat me badly with my reactions. When he lashed out, I would pursue him. When he gave me the silent treatment, I would pursue him. Every time he treated me with contempt, I would try harder to resolve things and would apologize for upsetting him. He always got what he wanted. He wanted to be pursued. If a baby throws a tantrum and gets his way, why would he ever stop throwing tantrums?

Floyd also helped me learn to accept that I could not avoid conflict by only using the perfect words. He explained that relationships are messy, but where there is mutual love and respect, you just clean up the mess. It's not about trying to be perfect and never making a mistake.

Then there were the really bizarre arguments.

After Dennis began his career with the lending institution, he went from feeling low and insecure to feeling arrogant and cocky. Financial success inflated his ego. At first, I thought it was great that he was feeling so good about himself again. But feeling good about himself always fed his narcissism in unhealthy ways. When he was feeling successful, he became a bully again rather quickly. He worked with brokers in the Nashville area, but he processed loans through an office in Atlanta, and he often went there for meetings. He liked for me to go with him, and if school interfered he'd get mad. So I tried to make sure I could go whenever invited.

On one of those trips, Dennis casually told me that Mike (not his real name), a married coworker, offered to take me to lunch so I wouldn't be stuck alone in a hotel room all day. Dennis said he was taking his loan processor (who was female) to lunch. I thought it was kind of strange that we couldn't just all go together, but it seemed to mean a lot to Dennis for me not to offend his coworker by turning down the invitation. I really wanted to stay in the room and study. But I knew that would be unacceptable. So I said I okay. I actually had a nice time with Mike. He was polite and pleasant. The restaurant he suggested was good. The conversation flowed easily and I wasn't uncomfortable with him as a person, but it was still weird.

The next trip to Atlanta coincided with our anniversary. (We had an anniversary in October and in March since we married twice. This was March of 2001.) We were going to extend our stay and celebrate our anniversary over the weekend. As I was packing for both of us, Dennis mentioned that he had committed me to another lunch date with Mike. I said I would rather not go and asked if he would please get me out of it. I wanted to stay in the room and study. And besides that, I told him I just didn't feel comfortable going to lunch alone with a married man.

Dennis insisted that I could not say no and offend his coworker. He emphasized how much Mike liked me and thought I was attractive, and envied Dennis for being married to me. I felt like I was being pimped out. I realized then it was all about Dennis' ego. I found his "request" unreasonable, but when he demanded I go, it was hurtful. It clearly communicated that I was an object to him. I had accepted the first invitation simply to be friendly and agreeable, but I drew the line at having a regular lunch date arranged for me by my own husband. Mike seemed nice enough, and the initial lunch date was fine. He was a perfect gentleman. But it wasn't him I had the problem with. It was Dennis. It was so demeaning to have my own husband insist that I go out to lunch with another guy just because he was envious of him. I was nothing more than an extension of Dennis and his ego. I was there to provide narcissistic supply. And when I refused, I was objectified and ridiculed. I stood my ground and

Dennis threatened to go to Atlanta without me if I wouldn't go to lunch with Mike. And that's what he did. He never called the whole weekend, in spite of it being our wedding anniversary. He completely dismissed my feelings and never made any attempt to understand them. He continued to insist that I was the one who had been unreasonable.

On another occasion, we went to California on business (to the corporate office) and extended our stay. Dennis was making money hand over fist, and we stayed at The Ritz Carlton in Laguna Niguel. We were going to see friends. As we were leaving the room to go work out first thing in the morning, I stepped over a newspaper in the doorway. "That is just like you," Dennis said in his most sarcastic tone.

Totally oblivious to what I'd done, I said, "What?"

"You are so selfish. Rather than picking the paper up for me, you intentionally step over it and leave it for me to pick up."

Nothing could have been further from the truth. I have always been somewhat oblivious by nature, and I simply did not *think* to pick up the newspaper. I certainly didn't do it to intentionally insult him. Had I been able to predict his reaction, you better believe I would not have stepped over the newspaper without picking it up for him. But I could not have predicted his reaction in a million years. It was absurd, but, of course, I did what I always did. I started apologizing and defending myself. But nothing satisfied him. It became a full blown character assassination.

The same man I had stood by for the last two torturous years, thinking he would appreciate me for all time because I had been so unselfish in my love for him, was annihilating me and my character for not picking up a stupid newspaper for him. In my attempts to defend my character, I said that I thought most people would expect a gentleman to pick something up off the floor for a lady and not the reverse. Well, that was the wrong thing to say. It only infuriated him more and things went further downhill from there. (Imagine the audacity of my implying that he was not a gentleman.)

In his anger Dennis told me that he was going to leave me for the day. I should have told him to take a hike and gone to the pool, but in my state of codependence, I thought the day would be ruined if he left me there. I cried. I pleaded with him not to stay mad. I apologized. I said it was thoughtless of me. I begged him not to hold a grudge all day when we were spending all this money and could be having a great time. He wouldn't even look at me while I groveled. But finally he said, "You can go with me if you want to. It's up to you." And I went. He was cold to me until late in the day. Then, when he got good and ready, he acted like nothing had happened. I was *grateful* that it was over, and I can't begin to tell you how many times this cycle played out.

Dennis loved to bait and antagonize me. It was so exhausting. One time in the early 2000s, following his major depression, he started in on me, telling me I did not appreciate him and was ungrateful. He kept taunting me until I couldn't take it anymore. Through tears of exasperation and anger, I yelled, "I hate you!" The minute he got that response (the response he was obviously looking for), he became icily calm and lowered his voice to a hushed tone for dramatic effect. He mocked me, saying softly, "Look at you. You're hysterical. You need help with your anger. You have a problem."

Dennis was intentionally cruel and condescending. And the worst pain was the contempt and constant belittling.

One night Dennis was sitting in his recliner watching TV and I was sitting across the room in the love seat reading. He had dropped the remote control and it was on the floor right next to his foot, but because he had a big blanket in his lap, he couldn't see it. He asked if I would get up and get it for him. "It is right next to your foot. All you have to do is lean forward," I pointed out.

"Come on, just get the remote for me," he demanded.

"You don't need me to get up and get it for you. It is right next to your foot." He wouldn't even glance at his foot.

He replied sarcastically, "But will you not get it for me just because I'm asking you to?"

"No. It's ridiculous that you are asking me to do it for you when all you have to do is lean over and get it yourself." I had gained some courage in counseling.

I was eating a bag of microwave popcorn. And when I didn't do what he wanted, he got up, walked over to me, took the bag of popcorn out of my hand, and dumped it on top of my head, laughing as he watched it fall all over me, the love seat, and the floor. "How does that feel?" And then he calmly walked out of the room, leaving the mess for me to clean up. He was displaying his power over me exactly the way he did when he shoved an ice cream bar in my face the first week of our marriage in 1975.

Nothing about him had changed. If anything, he was a bigger bully than he had ever been. But now it had nothing to do with depression.

༄

My counselor demonstrated my role in the relationship one day. He slammed a can of soda down onto a coffee table, and said, "This table is not a person but an object. It is there for my comfort and use; for me to do what I want with it. If I want to slam a can of soda down on it, it cannot say back to me 'that's cold' or 'that hurts.' It doesn't get to talk back or have feelings because it's an object. In your marriage to Dennis, you are the table."

What an effective illustration, I thought. Not because I needed my counselor to enlighten me about how I felt in the relationship. I certainly felt like an object. But his illustration defined me in a way that resulted in an epiphany. I was not only the table. I had offered myself as a table for all those years.

Chapter 10
BECAUSE HE CAN

"The abusive man's goal in a heated argument is in essence to get you to stop thinking for yourself and to silence you, because to him your opinions and complaints are obstacles to the imposition of his will as well as an affront to his sense of entitlement." —Lundy Bancroft

BY MID-2000, DENNIS WAS FEELING SO GOOD ABOUT himself, he claimed he no longer needed counseling and didn't have time for it. One of the conditions of getting back together back in October 1999 had been that we would continue in counseling as a maintenance plan. So when Dennis stopped going, I was disappointed. But at this point Dennis was dismissing Floyd's advice anyway. I didn't try to force him to go; I simply expressed my desire to continue alone. Dennis was fine with that because he thought I needed to talk to Floyd about my relationship with my dad and had suggested individual counseling to me months earlier.

My dad's second marriage ended in 1997, and he moved from California to Tennessee. He was having health challenges and was suffering from a minor bout of depression. I helped him recover from a difficult divorce and took him to specialists in Nashville to treat health issues resulting from newly diagnosed Parkinson's disease. I had spent a considerable amount of time trying to help him get healthy again while I was at the same time trying to help Dennis get through his deep depression. Dad steadily improved physically and emotionally, and we developed a closer relationship during this time.

One evening in 1999 my dad called and asked if we could go to breakfast early the next morning—just the two of us. I said, "Sure." The next morning when my dad showed up I was surprised to open the front door and see a young woman I knew standing next to him. It was a complete shock when he announced that we were not really going to breakfast; they were on their way to the courthouse to get married and hoped I would go with them as a witness. More shocking was that his bride was thirty-four years his junior. I was forty, and she was twenty-eight. They had met ten years earlier at a wedding and after reconnecting via the Internet and talking on the phone, Dad proposed that they should marry instead of dating. They were absolutely sure they wanted to be together. He believed that people in the church would never accept them dating, but they would have to accept them as a married couple.

I knew they were *both* making a big mistake. I tried to lovingly reason with them. We sat in my living room while I pointed out my concerns. Being unable to dissuade them, I agreed to serve as a witness as a demonstration of my unconditional love, as long as they wanted me there knowing I wasn't in agreement with their hasty union. They were both adults. I didn't want to control them. I wasn't even in opposition to them as a couple; I just knew they were moving way too fast. They said they understood my reservations, but still wanted me to be there.

My brothers took a strong stand against the marriage and my dad reacted badly. Following the wedding, he sent emails to *all of us*, threatening to move away and never see us again unless we embraced his new wife and loved her as he did. The emails represented still more undeserved rejection from my dad, and what made it so much worse was that I had already given my unconditional love *willingly*. There was no basis for him to give me an ultimatum. The marriage ended within a matter of months and then my dad immediately started calling me, expecting to receive sympathy and a listening ear. I was still feeling hurt by his words and actions. I resented him for expecting to cry on my shoulder after the way he'd treated me, but I felt guilty for feeling that way. Needless to say, I had some things to talk about in counseling.

Floyd helped me work through my wounds as a daughter since it was all so fresh at the time. However, I didn't need more than one or two sessions to put those issues in context and move on. After that, my ongoing counseling revolved around my marital struggles.

My counseling sessions were so helpful that I determined in my heart if Dennis ever tried to prevent me from continuing, I would refuse to give them up. But Dennis really had no excuse for me to stop going. By that time, he was making so much money he couldn't have possibly claimed we couldn't afford it. In fact, he would take great offense at the suggestion there was *anything* we could *not* afford. His material success was a source of great pride for him. Money was the only thing that really seemed to make Dennis feel he had value as a human being. And being a big spender demonstrated his worth. If I ever said, "Do you think we can afford this?" he would act insulted. And then he'd remind me of how much money he made.

On one of our trips to Atlanta in 2001, we planned some family time with my brother Chris and his family. We drove down together and checked into rooms at the same hotel. Dennis had a meeting at his branch office and then we took the kids to Six Flags. We were having a great day when suddenly the weather turned and it started to storm. So we had to take cover in a pavilion with a lot of other park guests until the rain stopped. There was a no smoking sign in the covered space and a young guy at the other end of this area lit up a cigarette. It annoyed Dennis, so he approached the guy, who was much younger and smaller than him, and instructed him to put out the cigarette. Probably thinking he was dealing with a pushover, the kid refused. Well, Dennis' temper flared, and he demanded the cigarette be put out. When the kid defied him again, Dennis grabbed him momentarily by the throat, and there was a minor scuffle before Dennis let go and walked away. The kid and his friends went straight to security. When they returned to the area, they confronted Dennis about his behavior. We had distracted the children as my brother, sister-in-law, and I realized the situation was getting ugly. We all knew Dennis had a volatile temper, but none of us had expected the altercation to become physical. I watched the whole scenario play out from beginning to end in horror. I was so embarrassed.

Dennis denied grabbing the kid and since there was no physical harm, security let him go. The astonishing thing is, when it was all over, Dennis said to me in amazement, "That guy accused me of grabbing him by the throat!"

"You *did* grab him by the throat."

He looked at me in disbelief and said, "I did?" He claimed he couldn't even remember doing it.

Dennis became agitated and nervous about further repercussions at that point. He couldn't stay at the park. He had to go back to the room. Although he was humble about it later, and obviously remorseful, we didn't talk about it again. I never heard him boast about this episode like he had others. I think it actually scared him that he'd not even realized what he'd done.

In 2001, we began the process of building a new home on property we had purchased in Greenbrier. Dennis was in a hurry to get started. But I had a bit of anxiety. The long depression ordeal had taken a huge toll on me emotionally. The memories were still very fresh. And I didn't want to get back into a heavy stress situation so quickly.

Having heard many people say they nearly divorced after going through the stress of building a home, I was concerned. I also expressed my concerns about taking on financial stress unnecessarily. Dennis was so confident he would continue making big money in the future, but I wasn't. I pointed out that the economy could change and affect his business. After many years in real estate, we had been through economic downturns. I told him that I thought it might be a good idea for us to wait and save so we could keep our house payment low. "Our marriage means more to me than having a bigger house," I said. "We live in a nice house already. I just want you to know I don't need a big fancy house to be happy."

"Well, it's not about *you*!" he shot back. "I work hard and earn a lot of money, and I want something to *show* for my hard work." The house was about his ego. I was disappointed, but I didn't want to fight. So I just dropped it. We broke ground on our dream home in April. And I was given full responsibility for managing the process. Dennis' exact words to me were: "My job is to earn the money to pay for it. Your job is everything else."

Building the dream house did become very stressful. Every time I tried to discuss a major decision with him, he would say "build it the way you want and don't worry about what it costs." That's not my personality. I was raised to be more conservative and to live within my means. Of course all the extras appealed to me, but as we exceeded our budget by thousands of dollars, I started to worry that we were overspending. Whenever I put off having some costly upgrade thinking we could do it later, Dennis would go around me and tell our contractor to go ahead and do it now. I really wasn't in charge of anything. I realized later that I was just the fall guy when we ultimately went one hundred thousand dollars over our initial budget.

One Sunday morning we were planning to go shopping for light fixtures. Out of the blue Dennis announced that he was tired of getting calls from telemarketers and wanted me to write a letter requesting that we be put on a do not call list. I told him I would do it Monday, so we could get on with our plans for the day. He said sternly, "No. I want you to do it right now."

"It's Sunday. It can't even go out in the mail before tomorrow. Can I at least type it up tonight after we get back?"

"No. I know you. You won't remember to do it tonight or tomorrow. I want it done now." His request was unreasonable, and I hated being treated like his slave. I asked why he was making such an issue out of something that was clearly not urgent and did not need to be done right that minute. He blew up. He yelled. He slammed doors so hard that pictures fell off of walls. And then he announced that he was leaving. "You can go pick out light fixtures by yourself!" He was unreasonable with or without heavy stress being a factor, but the stress of our mounting building costs seemed to be taking a toll.

Our contractor would ask me for money periodically as different sub-contractors completed their work. We had a construction loan, but we also were using our own cash because of all the upgrades, so sometimes I would have to ask Dennis if he was going to be closing any loans and getting a big paycheck. Since I was in charge of paying our bills and managing the checking account, I needed to know how much money he expected to receive and keep him informed about the amount that was going out, but he resented having to talk about it when the money wasn't there. He would say, "I don't know how I can possibly earn more money!" as if I was suggesting his income was inadequate.

If I tried to have a conversation about paying contractors in the morning, he'd blow up at me and demand that I not bring up the subject right before he was trying to start his work day. I was setting a bad tone for his day. If I tried to have a conversation in the evening, he'd blow up and say he needed to be able to relax to get a good night's sleep. If I met him for lunch, he'd insist on being able to enjoy his meal. After weeks of trying to get him to talk about the finances, in exasperation I said, "You know, I've tried to have this conversation with you morning, noon, and night. Obviously timing isn't the issue. You just don't want to have a conversation about the costs of this house. But I'm stuck in the middle between you and the builder, and I don't have a choice." He got furious and the conversation ended in another fight.

In January of 2002, our son was getting serious with a young woman named Rebecca, who became his bride the following August. Dennis and I had been invited to her mother and step-father's home to watch the Super Bowl. During halftime, Rebecca's father and step-mother stopped by so that we could all meet one another. On the way home, Dennis expressed amazement that Rebecca's parents would agree to be in the same room with each other since they were divorced and remarried to other people. I didn't find that so odd and said that I thought it was great for the kids' sake. He said, "Well, if you and I ever get divorced, I will never agree to be in the same room with you and another guy." I chuckled because that attitude was so Dennis. That he would project himself into that situation and make such a declaration wasn't at all surprising.

But at that point I didn't have any expectation that we would ever be divorced again.

This *should have been* a great time in our lives. I was thrilled about having a daughter-in-law. I looked forward to one day having grandchildren. And I was proud of the man Danny was becoming. His engagement brought me nothing but pride and joy. I had a hard time understanding why the same things would not bring Dennis joy as well. Dennis was making more money than ever, which I thought would make him happy. He had assured me he would be *proud* of me for getting my degree, and I was excelling in my studies in college. We were building the beautiful new home he had wanted so much. It seemed to me like all the pieces that needed to be in place for a happier time in our life were there, yet Dennis was always mad about something. If only he were capable of happiness! He still had ugly flares of anger over the most minor issues in spite of so much potential. But I had convinced myself it wasn't that bad by comparing it to the two years of his deep depression. Anything would have seemed minor in comparison to that. What I did not comprehend at the time was how much Dennis was experiencing Danny's impending marriage as a loss of control. Floyd helped me eventually to understand when a person like Dennis feels threatened with this kind of power loss, the agitation, frustration and rage are transferred to someone else—usually the spouse or significant other. Although I believed we possessed every ingredient for happiness, it seemed that I was experiencing his antagonism and rage more than ever.

I had counseling appointments every other week. And I almost always had some kind of conflict to discuss. I would share with Floyd what happened and how I responded to it. And he would either validate my response as healthy or help me see where I had gone wrong. There was one rare break in the action, which I remember vividly. Dennis went two weeks without blowing up over anything and I felt like I had won the lottery. I showed up for my scheduled session in a euphoric state and told Floyd I wasn't even sure why I had kept my appointment. I was blissfully happy. Things were great. I had no problems and nothing to talk about. He asked, "What is the reason behind your being so blissfully happy?" And I proudly shared that Dennis had not picked a fight with me in two whole weeks. Not one single blow up! Floyd looked sad, which confused me. And then he asked, "You are blissfully happy simply because you haven't fought in two weeks?"

"Floyd, all I want is peace. That is all it takes to make me happy."

And he said flatly, "Do you ever really have peace?"

I just looked at him. I felt like he was throwing a big wet blanket on my euphoria. It almost irritated me. I wanted him to let me enjoy my temporary bliss. But he wouldn't. His job was to make me think about what I was revealing. He then explained to me that a lack of conflict is not the same as peace. He asked me if Dennis still had mood swings, if his positive feelings toward me could turn instantly negative at any given moment. Hadn't I experienced moments and days of being valued before and then been devalued and objectified in the blink of an eye over something minor? Was the bliss and so-called peace only because of my effort toward not rocking the boat? If that was the case, then it would be wrong to label what I felt as real peace. He was so right in everything he said and I knew it. I wanted him to refrain from bursting my joyful bubble, even if it was quite temporary, but I knew it was his job to help me face reality.

I recently read the book *The Gift of Fear* by Gavin De Becker. I recognized myself in De Becker's description of a battered woman: "Like the battered child, the battered woman gets a powerful feeling of overwhelming relief when an incident ends. She becomes addicted to that feeling. The abuser is the only person who can deliver moments of peace, by being his better self for a while. Thus, the abuser holds the key to the abused person's feeling of well-being." Reading this gave me additional insight into my euphoria.

Two weeks is a long time to someone who is grateful for mere moments.

ຈ

During the years Dennis was so successful as an account executive with the mortgage company in Atlanta, I accompanied him on several business trips. On one occasion, the company Dennis worked for held a function at The Peabody Hotel in Memphis. We met a group of Dennis' business colleagues for dinner. It came up in conversation that Dennis and I had been divorced and remarried. Somebody asked how we had gotten back together. Dennis started telling them, with me sitting there listening, that we had broken up because he'd gone through a midlife crisis, went wild and crazy for a time (obviously inferring womanizing), and I had waited patiently for him to come to his senses. He added how grateful he was for my ability to forgive. He really played it up, making me sound so long-suffering. It was nauseatingly distasteful. It was a performance of grandiosity. He was going out of his way to portray himself as some big player and me as the "stand by your man" wife, waiting for him to see the error of his ways and come home. It was a complete lie, and it was degrading to watch his face light up in front of his audience as he talked about himself going through this phase of his life. It was unnecessary and disrespectful to me as his wife. He did live the life of a player while we were divorced, but that wasn't why we divorced and I didn't sit around waiting for him to come home. He actually begged me to take him back. I did not, however, challenge him in front of his colleagues. I sat there and let him have the stage he was obviously enjoying.

Floyd had been stressing to me in counseling that I needed to confront Dennis more often about how his behavior impacted me, even if it meant rocking the boat and suffering consequences. Floyd had helped me see that by placating Dennis and trying to avoid upsetting him all the time, even choosing the words that would be most palatable for him rather than the words that described best how I felt, I was facilitating his bad behavior. What I viewed as noble, self-sacrificing behavior as a wife was actually quite the opposite. I was protecting myself constantly. I wasn't helping Dennis, and I wasn't pleasing God. In fact, I was "enabling ungodly behavior" as Floyd put it. I was motivated by my need to avoid unpleasant consequences and protect myself from his angry responses. As I came to accept that I had such a distinct role in perpetuating my abuse through accepting and enabling his behavior, I became motivated to resist these tendencies, and become a healthier person. One of the first ways I tried to change was by telling the truth instead of doing cart wheels to avoid it.

I still tried to choose my words ever so carefully, but I chose to tell the truth rather than placate Dennis. The night at the Peabody, after we went back to our room, I told Dennis how much his behavior had hurt and embarrassed me. And I asked him why he lied to his coworkers and made up a story about his philandering while I waited around for him to outgrow the behavior. He blew up and told me off, of course. It was so ugly that I picked up a book and went to the lounge of the hotel, where I sat in a chair listening to piano music and reading for hours. I did not return to the room until after midnight because the thought of being in the same room with Dennis produced so much anxiety for me.

※

We moved into our new home in May of 2002. I had spent an entire year building this home and had no idea that I would only live there for three months. Things were not going well in our marriage. I could feel myself shutting down emotionally. I wasn't depressed. It was more like I was checking out. Dennis was becoming more and more difficult to get along with no matter how hard I tried to stay out of his way. He continually tried to bait and antagonize me. He seemed to enjoy it. I tend to be a reactive person emotionally, so I played right into his hands most of the time. But I was growing so weary of the endless games.

Danny and Rebecca were to be married on August 3, and I was trying to get the house as organized as possible because friends of ours from another state were planning to stay with us. Dennis didn't help me at all. He did not have a physically demanding job. His motto was always that he worked smart, not hard. When he was home, he was either sitting in his recliner watching TV or sitting in his office watching TV. Still, he refused to help pack or unpack boxes. After all, he earned the money, and I did everything else.

Dennis rarely ever got out of his chair to help me with anything. When I came home with groceries, he pretended not to hear when I called for help. He would step over a full trash bag that I set by the door to be taken out rather than take it out for me. I had to pack everything for him when we traveled, and he would flat-out say, "I'm not helping." When I was doing

100 percent of the packing to move, he would sit in his recliner and ask me to take a break and make him a sandwich or get him a Diet Coke rather than get out of his chair. I remember the night before the movers came. I had to stay up into the wee hours of the morning packing because everything had to be ready to go when they arrived at 8:00 a.m. Dennis had fallen asleep in his recliner watching TV as I worked. He woke up, walked past me and said, "Well, you may choose to stay up all night, but I don't. I'm going to bed." I told him I didn't have a choice. It had to be done by morning. And he said he was glad it wasn't *his job* to pack. He laughed mockingly as he left the room.

When my sister-in-law, Cheryl, and I went to pick up a van load of clothes, I made trip after trip up three flights of stairs, lugging his clothes and mine to the master bedroom closet, along with many other miscellaneous items. I had called him on the phone to say we had picked up the last few things and asked if he'd be willing to come out and help carry them in. His terse response was, "Nope. Won't be doing that. I'm busy working." (He was sitting in his office watching TV.) And to add insult to injury, when I said "Okay," he got indignant and told me not to get short with him. I couldn't win no matter what I said or did. It seemed like he just enjoyed being a jerk.

After that I didn't ask for help again. I just kept working on getting things in place. One Sunday afternoon, he wanted me to watch a movie with him. I was in the middle of unpacking boxes and doing laundry, so I asked if he'd mind my finishing what I was doing and watching it with him later on. He wanted me to stop what I was doing and watch it right then. It wasn't an invitation. It was a test, a demand over something inconsequential. It wasn't as if he asked me to stop and do something important. He asked me to sit down and watch a movie. I said, "I can't. I've got so much to do." He got mad, but I tried to let it roll off my back.

Just an hour or so later, my sister-in-law called. She had bought two dresses for Danny's wedding and couldn't decide which one to keep. She wanted to come over and get my opinion. Without giving it a second thought, I said, "Of course! Come on over." Dennis answered the door, and without any greeting or pleasantries, he pointed to the stairs. She came up to the bedroom and tried on the dresses. I told her which one I liked. We talked for a few minutes before she said she felt like she should leave because Dennis obviously didn't want her there. I told her not to pay attention to him. He was just pouting (again). After she left, I tried to act like nothing had happened. But Dennis wouldn't speak to me.

Danny and Rebecca came by, and we were talking in the upstairs bedroom when Dennis came into the doorway. He announced he was going for a drive, and asked the kids if he could bring anything back for them to eat. He acted like I wasn't even there. He never looked at me or spoke to me or asked if I wanted anything. He directed his comments only to Danny and Rebecca. When he returned, I asked what he was so upset about. And he informed me that he thought it was telling that I could not stop what I was doing to watch a movie with him, but I could drop everything for Cheryl. I told him he was acting like a child. For that offense he gave me the silent treatment for two full weeks. He also slept in the guest room to make it more official.

The tension in the house was so thick you could, as they say, cut it with a knife. I couldn't stand being in my own home. In the evening I'd go over to Chris and Cheryl's just to be somewhere else and have someone to talk to. I would stay late, and when I'd pull into my garage at night, a wave of anxiety flooded over my whole body. I hated going home. I was so tense that I knew I couldn't immediately sleep, so I'd get in my spa tub, turn on the jets, and just soak until I started feeling sleepy. Then I'd go to bed.

Dennis stayed in his office with the door closed when he was home. One day I finally confronted him and asked if we could talk about what was going on. He told me that he felt like our marriage was going off the tracks, and he believed it was because ever since his depression I no longer respected him. He said that it wasn't fair for me to lose respect for him over his depression because depression was an illness, and he could not help what had happened to him. (He apparently forgot admitting to me that he deliberately manipulated me with the depression.) He felt like I was throwing it in his face every time I made even a slight reference to those two years. He felt like I would never forget or let him forget. Instead he wanted to pretend it had never happened. He said he could not deal with the lack of respect he felt from me, explaining that how I made him feel as a man was "paramount" for him. (His feelings were my responsibility.) Respect was something he absolutely needed to have from his wife.

I could hear Floyd's counsel in my mind at that moment. He had told me that when I apologized and begged for Dennis' forgiveness as an attempt to smooth things over, I had actually been acting in an unhealthy way. I told Floyd that I didn't want to be unhealthy anymore. Once I learned that my behavior was feeding his, I knew I had to change. Floyd had asked me if I wanted to be healthy enough to risk the marriage, explaining that healthy responses would be met with great resistance and be unacceptable to Dennis. He said there was a small chance that Dennis could respond by wanting to work on himself, but there was a much greater chance the marriage would rapidly crash and burn when I committed to changing my enabling ways. I told him I was ready to risk the marriage.

So when Dennis demanded my respect, I remembered Floyd's advice; I knew I had to resist the impulse to say what I thought Dennis wanted to hear. I knew I had to tell him the truth whether he could handle it or not. I had to be completely honest and accept the fallout. I calmly explained to him that I also wanted to be able to respect my husband. It was just as important to me as it was to him. I kept my tone gentle and chose my words carefully. "Dennis, I'm not going to lie to you. Although I have not lost *all* respect for you, I agree that I don't respect you the way I want to respect you as my husband. But it is not because you went through a depression. It's the way you treat me. I did lose respect for you when, after two years of standing by you and caring for your every need during the depression, you hit me in the face for not responding the way you wanted me to, and threatened to kill yourself as a means to hurt and punish me. I forgive you, but, no matter how much you might want me to, I simply can't erase the pain from my memory as if it never happened. You promised to treat me differently so I would come home. But you have not kept your promise. Giving me the silent treatment and sleeping in the other room for not dropping everything to watch a movie with you is childish; not at all the behavior of a grown man. It's your *behavior* I cannot respect. So unless you only want the kind of respect that is demanded from a subordinate in the military, you need to behave in a way that inspires genuine, *heartfelt* respect. I can't manufacture that." Needless to say he didn't like my answer.

Immediately he turned it around to me and started to make ugly remarks about how I'd been coming home late and getting in the bathtub. "Do you think I don't know what's going on when you come home late at night and immediately take a bath? I'm not stupid." His voice dripped with sarcasm and his face conveyed disgust. I knew what he was implying.

He was accusing me of having an affair. It was his way of reaching back and throwing my past in my face. I did not believe he actually thought I was having an affair. He just wanted to hurt me as badly as he could for being that honest. Floyd had been right. Change was unacceptable.

The next day, I walked into Dennis' office. The fourteen pages he said he would keep forever were torn into little pieces. Half of it was discarded in a trash bag. The other half was on the floor probably to make sure I saw it. All hope of ever being treated differently died in me that day. He was telling me in a tangible way that my wounded heart meant nothing to him.

I discussed this with Floyd in my next counseling session.

"Shari, do you know why Dennis treats you the way he does?"

"No. I don't."

"Because he can."

Chapter 11
THE WEDDING / THE DIVORCE

"Detachment doesn't mean you don't let the experience penetrate you. On the contrary, you let it penetrate you fully. That's how you are able to leave it." —Mitch Albom

THE WEEK OF MY SON'S WEDDING WAS A MIXTURE OF the best and the worst of times. I had always looked forward to the day Danny would marry the most important woman in his life. Yes, you read that correctly. I never considered myself the most important woman in Danny's life. He was in my care for a little while, and I'm a significant part of his life, but the most important woman God would give to Danny would come later. And that reality was never threatening to me.

Some mothers wish they could keep their sons little forever, but I never had that desire. I enjoyed him at every stage of his life and always believed we would have a great adult relationship. I did not feel like I was losing him. I was thrilled to be gaining a daughter. I recognized early in their relationship that Rebecca was a gift from God to my son and also to me and that God did not intend for a son to put his mother ahead of his wife. Because of the mother-in-law experiences I'd had, I knew all the things I never wanted to do to my new daughter-in-law long before Danny ever met her, and I believe if a mother knows her rightful place and shows the proper respect for her daughter-in-law, a lot of unnecessary conflict and resentment can be avoided. My hopes and dreams were for a close relationship with both of them in all the years to come. And one of the highest priorities of my life was to never bring stress to their married life with parental demands and expectations. As I wrote in an earlier chapter, I wanted only to enhance their lives with my unconditional love. For all of my unhealthy ways as a wife, I believed I knew how to navigate this new relationship in a healthy way.

My daughter-in-law is a strong woman. I have admired her from the day I met her. I don't remember her ever cowering in Dennis' presence. And that impressed me. I could feel her strength and recognized that she was not intimidated by his sarcasm. I believe Dennis sensed that too. Even though he liked her very much, it was apparent to me that she was an irritation to him. It had nothing to do with her personally. It boiled down to two things: he saw her as taking Danny away from him and he had no power over her. I think he was afraid Rebecca would encourage independence in Danny. That was the last thing *he* wanted, but that made *me* love her all the more.

From the time Danny was small, Dennis lavished a lot of nice *things* on Danny. He always had the best basketball shoes, the latest video games, and we took a lot of fun trips. Danny was a big Magic Johnson fan, and we took him to many Laker games at the Los Angeles Forum. We even took him to various parts of the country to visit different major league baseball parks because he loved baseball. Danny was an only child and we went crazy buying him presents at Christmas. So in the eyes of many, Danny was spoiled and adored. But what people couldn't always see was the constant pressure on Danny to keep his dad "filled up" emotionally. A narcissist has an excessive and constant need for attention and adoration that does not take into account the feelings, opinions or preferences of other people. A kid should not feel responsible for their parents' emotions. It's too heavy a load for small shoulders.

Danny has shared with me many times how he never felt he was permitted to say no to his dad in even the smallest ways. If he was playing Nintendo and his dad stuck his head in the door to ask, "Would you like to ride along with me to look at property?" the only acceptable response was "Yes." If he told the truth and said that looking at property was boring and he'd rather play video games, his dad would have pouted for the rest of the day and acted like Danny had rejected him. Danny would then feel guilty. Danny was emotionally manipulated from the time he was born. The message was clear. He was supposed to meet his dad's emotional needs at all times. He couldn't make his dad sad or mad. It was exactly what Dennis' mother had done to him, which he resented, and it is what Dennis did to us. We learned that it was our job to provide adoration. It's not always conscious. It was like we had developed an emotional thermometer and were constantly taking Dennis' emotional temperature, and even other people's temperature in other relationships. The role of trying to make sure everyone is okay and happy and getting along is hard enough for an adult, let alone a child.

Dennis didn't have a lot to give emotionally. He needed others to fill him up. And he didn't have much guidance or wisdom to offer his son. He was not a mentor or a role model, but he could buy a lot of nice things for his son. It made him happy seeing his son enjoying those things, but that his son had the best of everything fed his ego and made him feel like a success. This also served as another way for him to inflict guilt on both Danny and me whenever he did not get what he wanted from us emotionally. Dennis said the same kinds of things to Danny that he said to me. He took sarcastic jabs at us with his "It must be rough . . ." remarks, intended to make us feel ungrateful for the things we enjoyed that his money bought for us.

This spoiling of Danny continued into high school. Dennis bought a vehicle for Danny when he turned sixteen. Danny was not expected to pay for his car or car insurance. I don't remember if Danny ever had to buy his own gas. Dennis wanted Danny to date more in high school, so he offered to pay for dates, holding up a wad of cash. When Danny's vehicle needed an oil change or a tire, Dennis would offer the keys to his own car and say, "Here, drive my Lexus to school, and I'll take care of it." This made him feel like a hero. It also was Dennis' way of keeping Danny dependent on him. Losing Danny would mean losing one of his emotional supports.

I am not suggesting Dennis wasn't trying to be a good dad. I believe he was, but he was in the only ways he knew how, with material gifts since he had nothing to give emotionally or spiritually. And, of course, Dennis' ego played into it too. By doing everything for his son, Dennis kept him depending on his father. He always wanted Danny to rely on him; he always wanted to have an important place in Danny's life. Whenever I privately protested his making everything easier for Danny, telling him that he needed to encourage Danny to be independent, he'd say, "Shut up and mind your own business."

Dennis even enabled Danny's lax attitude toward school. He didn't think Danny's grades were important. He didn't encourage him to study hard. But he praised him any time Danny was successfully able to "work the system." Most high school boys find ways to get around things or charm a teacher now and then. Danny was no exception, and he'll be the first to tell you that. Any time Danny shared a successful con story, his dad beamed. When he was not depressed and fearfully attending church, Dennis believed rules were meant to be broken.

I had completely different convictions. I thought it was important not to skip class. I thought it was important to study and get good grades. I thought it was important for Danny to become independent and self-sufficient. As often as I could, I would try to instill my principles and values in my son. Of course these heart-to-heart talks occurred when Dennis wasn't around. And I'm sure that Danny regarded many of them as lectures. I could always tell when he was simply enduring my admonitions because he wouldn't respond. He would listen and shake his head in agreement, just waiting for the talk to end. It was a tactic he learned from my youngest brother. If he sat in silence and just listened, he knew I would get tired of the sound of my own voice more quickly and the lecture would be over. He knew at an early age that I didn't have any support from Dennis when it came to his grades. A mother can only have so much influence when the father minimizes and undermines her values.

Don't think that Dennis didn't love his son. I believe he did. He just did so in the only way he knew how, with a selfish, consuming, entitled love. He was not capable of loving unselfishly. It had nothing to do with Danny or me. It was the way he'd been raised. He was trained to be emotionally selfish. Floyd lifted so much emotional baggage off of me when he told me, "Shari, Dennis would have treated any wife the way he's treated you. As imperfect and flawed as you are, his behavior has nothing to do with you as a person. You could not have been a good enough wife to avoid this behavior or make him happy. It's about him."

So when Danny became engaged to a strong young woman who showed no signs of being easily manipulated by Dennis, I was thrilled. I believed this could only be liberating for my son.

※

The week of the wedding was exciting and turbulent for me. It was August 2002, and Dennis and I were not getting along well at all. As hard as that was, I was determined not to let Dennis rob me of my joy. I was looking forward to the bridal luncheon, the rehearsal dinner, the wedding, and the reception. They were once in a lifetime events, and I wanted to be focused on the moment for all of them. Dennis was not speaking to me again just days before the wedding. I can't even remember why he wasn't speaking, but I had learned that he had tried to sabotage my relationship with my own son, and I was angry.

Dennis and I were giving Danny and Rebecca a trip to Hawaii as their wedding gift. We were also hosting a nice rehearsal dinner. Even though Dennis was making great money, we were under a lot of financial stress at the time. In addition to the payments on our construction loan, we had put almost one hundred thousand dollars cash into the dream house. Dennis blew through money like there was no tomorrow. Spending money fed his ego. He felt that his role was to earn money and receive praise for doing it well. I was the one who managed the checkbook and paid the bills, and if more money was spent than earned, that was my problem. And looking at our budget, I thought a honeymoon in Hawaii was a generous wedding gift. I enjoyed doing things for Danny, but I thought there should be limits. Dennis wasn't big on limitations, and the way he attempted to sabotage my relationship with Danny was by offering him cash spending money for his honeymoon on the condition that it would remain their secret. Dennis had never discussed offering spending money with me, and he didn't want me to know. I believe he saw it as a chance to look like the more generous parent in Danny's eyes. He wanted to be the hero who couldn't do enough for his son. I was convinced then, as I am now, that Dennis was jealous of my relationship with Danny. While Danny was young, he and Dennis had more in common. They were the guys, and he wanted to be Danny's buddy. Dennis was more indulgent as a parent than I was. I had a tendency to say no a lot more than Dennis did. I wasn't raised by parents who tried to be my buddy. They were just my parents. So I was the disciplinarian, the one who tried to set limits, especially during Danny's early years. But as Danny got older and entered high school, we developed an emotional closeness that his dad never had. Danny could talk to me about almost anything, and he would seek me out for deeper conversations. He asked for my opinions. Parents should never be in competition for their children's loyalty, but I think Dennis felt that he couldn't compete with the emotional bond between Danny and me, so he tried to make up for it with material things.

Danny wound up confessing to me that he had at first accepted the cash, but he had learned in premarital counseling that one of the worst mistakes in marriage is keeping financial secrets. He ended up telling his dad that he couldn't take the money if I couldn't know about it. And he wanted me to know exactly what had happened because he believed Dennis might eventually try to hurt me by putting his own slant on Danny's response. Danny knew his dad was capable of trying to sabotage our relationship and didn't want that to happen. Because I am a trusting person who rarely anticipates underhanded behavior, I was actually surprised (in spite of the condition of our marriage). I was thankful to know the truth because it compelled *me* to face the reality that Dennis was not above trying to sabotage my relationship with my own son. Facing this reality was extremely painful for me.

I told Danny I wasn't going to say anything to his dad about my knowledge of this before he and Rebecca left for their honeymoon. I didn't want any repercussions to tarnish the weekend. Since Dennis was giving me the silent treatment and I was feeling so betrayed, I decided to book a hotel room close to the church (our house was an hour away). In my mind, the marriage was just about over, and I wanted to give myself some much needed emotional space.

The Friday morning before the wedding I rehearsed what I was going to say to Dennis in the shower. Dennis was still lying in bed when I got out. I wrapped a towel around myself, walked over to him, and said, "I've reserved a hotel room for tonight and tomorrow night. I want to get through this weekend as a couple for Danny and Rebecca's sake. I intend to treat you warmly and respectfully and show no indication that anything is wrong. But once we get through the weekend I think we need to file for divorce. If we stay together, we are just going to wind up hating each other. And I don't want that." With no emotion he stated, "I couldn't agree more." I calmly suggested we meet at the church for the rehearsal and then ride to the rehearsal dinner in the same car. I did not want anyone to pick up on the strain between the two of us. He said, "Fine." Then I finished getting ready and left.

I called Floyd from my cell phone after I left. I was furious and told Floyd about Dennis offering Danny money behind my back. It was such a betrayal that I was done with Dennis. Floyd, who had never urged me to leave the marriage, told me that what Dennis had done was wrong, but it was a reason to have a conversation, not a reason to end the marriage. He insisted that I needed to confront Dennis and tell him how I felt. And he admitted that our marriage might not survive its challenges. But that offense wasn't the reason to file for divorce. I agreed to have a conversation with Dennis but wanted to wait until after the kids were in Hawaii to spare them any fallout. I knew Dennis was going to be mad at Danny for telling me.

The first event of the day was the bridal luncheon. I tried so hard to control my emotions. My world was collapsing and expanding simultaneously. The sorrow did not outweigh the joy, but I'm an emotional person and had to fight back the tears several times. I thought I held myself together fairly well under the circumstances.

Back at my hotel room while getting ready for the rehearsal and rehearsal dinner, I was looking forward to a nice night with Cheryl and my two nieces. I had invited them to spend the night at the hotel with me. I wanted the company, and I also thought it would make it easier to get the girls ready in the morning. They were in the wedding and wanted Aunt Shari to do their hair. So I had that to look forward to after the rehearsal dinner.

When I met Dennis at the church for the rehearsal, God infused me with the strength that only God can give. I was fully engaged with the joy and excitement of my son's special weekend. Dennis didn't matter. He was just there. I walked through the entry and right up to a group of people that included Dennis. I would describe myself as a great actress that evening, but I wasn't acting at all. I was myself. I was relaxed and completely taking in the moment. It seemed to surprise Dennis when I walked up smiling and speaking to him in a warm, friendly tone.

We rode together to the dinner as a couple just as we'd planned. Neither of us mentioned the conversation from that morning. I was so natural and at ease the whole evening, I think he wondered if I'd changed my mind. I posed for family pictures with a sense that they would be our last. I love looking at pictures from that night. You would never suspect from the photographs that I was under any stress at all. Thanks to God and a great photographer, I look radiantly happy in those pictures. And I truly was. It was one of the best nights of my life. There were so many laughs and such nice things said about the new couple by their friends and family. I was able to speak from my heart as well. I sat next to Dennis for only the first few minutes and then I was up mixing and mingling the majority of the time. I only returned to my assigned seat for the official parts of the evening.

The morning of the wedding my thoughts were completely focused on the ceremony, getting the girls and myself ready. Again, I was bursting with joy and pride and it shows in all the pictures. You can't fake that. Everything went beautifully, and after greeting several guests, I grabbed a plate of food and sat down next to Dennis at a table with friends in the reception hall. As soon as I sat down, I realized I had forgotten to pick up a drink. So I jumped up and went back for a glass of tea. When I returned, Dennis furrowed his brow as if I had slighted him. He said, "Well, here I thought you were going to get that for me." He was dead serious. He thought I should have noticed that he needed a refill. In spite of everything that was going on, he was surprised that I had not served him a drink instead of getting one for myself! I laughed and said, "Well, you were wrong." It felt so good.

The whole day I felt good, like I already was free from Dennis. In a moment of feeling sorry for Dennis the night before, I had told him he could stay in the hotel room with me after the wedding was over. Close friends of both of ours had come from out of state for the wedding and were staying in the same hotel as me. We were all going to dinner together after the wedding, and it just felt like the right thing to do at the time to invite Dennis to sleep at the hotel instead of having to drive home (an hour from where the wedding was held). I was so caught up in doing what I perceived as the *right* things, even to my own detriment. I was floating on air the entire day right up until Danny and Rebecca got in their getaway car and drove off to spend two nights at the Opryland Hotel. When they did, I felt like my insides were imploding, and I could hardly hold myself together. I was back in my hellish reality. Although internalizing my emotions only magnified them, I knew I could not confront Dennis about his betrayal for two more days. And in that moment I felt utterly alone.

When we got back to the hotel that night, I tried to sleep and could not. I couldn't stop crying. I wasn't making any noise, but the tears were flowing like a river. Dennis was snoring loudly and completely oblivious to my restlessness. I got up as quietly as I could and retreated to the comfort of a hot bath, and cried some more. I cried off and on all the next day. But it wasn't sadness that Danny and Rebecca had left. It wasn't empty nest sadness. It was the heaviness of my situation and *the emptiness of being with Dennis.*

I'm sure Dennis was confused by my cordial attitude all weekend and my invitation to share my hotel room. I'm sure there were times he believed I had changed my mind and didn't really want a divorce. He was mistaken. There was a huge emotional distance between us in spite of my hospitality. We were not a couple. I had just risen above our problems so well. He knew I was no actress and couldn't have faked my way through any of those events. I am a very transparent person. He knew I had to be as okay as I seemed, but when it was all over, all I could do was cry. I don't think he knew what to do or how to react. We didn't say much the next morning. He left for home first, and I told him I'd be there later. We were in separate vehicles and I was in no hurry. When we were both back home, we just avoided each other in the big house we had built. But he wasn't giving me the silent treatment for a change. I was the one avoiding him. I was the one setting the tone. I just didn't have anything to say to him.

Danny and Rebecca had another night at the hotel. Then we were supposed to pick them up and take them to the airport, so I had to put this conversation on hold for just a little while longer. After they departed for Hawaii, I confronted Dennis about offering cash to Danny behind my back. Of course, Dennis just got mad. He refused to acknowledge that he'd done anything wrong. And if I had a problem with anything he did, it was my problem. He also attacked Danny and spitefully informed me that Danny took the money and probably only told me because he felt guilty that he'd wanted to accept it and couldn't. (Danny's concern was validated. Dennis tried to put a spiteful slant on the situation.) He suggested that possibly Rebecca had convinced him he shouldn't. His words were dripping with resentment and hostility. There was absolutely no remorse on his part. It was a long, tense week.

There had been many times before when I felt like I was at the end of my rope, but this was different. I was dangling by a thread. I was forty-three years old. I had spent almost twenty-seven years beating my head against a brick wall. And at that moment, it felt like I had wasted the best years of my life on a man who was not even my friend. I began to weigh my options carefully. I was fearful of striking out on my own. I wasn't confident. I wasn't self-assured. I was flat out scared to death. And I wasn't sure what God expected of me. But there were a few things I felt certain of.

Dennis was more impossible to get along with now than he was when I married him. And he remained completely unwilling to look at himself or examine his priorities. Everything was always someone else's fault—usually mine. He had sent an intentional message that I didn't matter by tearing up the fourteen pages he vowed to keep forever as a reminder of how his behavior made me feel, which was extremely significant to me and powerful evidence that change would never happen. I believed that staying with Dennis could potentially shorten my life because of the toll the heavy stress was taking on me physically. I knew I was about to hit midlife and menopause. I knew there would be no compassion if I struggled the way some women do and I couldn't imagine what that would be like as his wife. I concluded that if the marriage was hopeless, no matter how hard it was to start over at age forty-three, it would be easier at forty-three than at fifty-three. I couldn't change the years I'd already given up, but I could refuse to throw away the next ten. And the final argument in my own mind for it being the ideal time to leave was simply that Dennis was at the pinnacle of haughtiness. He had an air of needing nothing, including me. I knew I was incapable of leaving him when he was down and out. That is partly why I hung in there for the two-year-long psychosis the way I did. I am not someone who abandons people in need.

It was the perfect opportunity. Dennis was feeling like king of the world. He was arrogant and condescending. He was making hundreds of thousands of dollars a year. He felt powerful and successful and superior. And in my heart, I knew this would not last forever. I knew his cycles. I knew eventually another depression would come. I knew his priorities and choices were self-destructive. And if I didn't take this window of opportunity while he was on top of the world, I might never have the same chance again. I could only justify leaving when he was so eager to show me that he didn't need me one bit. And that was the deciding factor in my decision. Now was the time.

We slept in separate rooms, and things were tense between us following the fight about the money. I had a lot to think about and I knew I needed to have a plan. The next steps would take a tremendous amount of courage on my part. I sensed that Dennis was confused about my behavior. I had said before the wedding that we needed to divorce, but I hadn't acted on that yet. It was like he was waiting and watching, trying to figure out where things stood. Through the years, divorce had come up in conversation and yet I had always stayed. I'm sure he doubted that I would follow through this time as well.

Floyd convinced me to have one more conversation with Dennis and to tell him exactly how I was feeling in the marriage before leaving. He said, "Don't put it into words that are palatable for Dennis like you always try to do. Use the words that describe how you really feel." I did not want to have this conversation because I knew it was pointless. I knew Dennis couldn't care less about how I felt. I knew there would be no compassion. And my anxiety was at an all-time high. It felt like going before a firing squad. But I forced myself to approach him because I never disregarded Floyd's advice.

It was two weeks after the wedding on a Sunday afternoon. Dennis was sitting in his recliner watching TV as I entered the room. I asked if we could talk, and he said, "What do you want?" I told him that obviously things had deteriorated badly between us and that neither of us was happy. I was in tears and was trembling, not because I was afraid of him physically, but because I knew how he was going to react, and it is painful to be treated like dirt by someone you've sacrificed so much for. I told him I had done a lot of thinking since the wedding. I didn't *want* to divorce, but I couldn't keep living this way. Then I forced myself to say the words, "I feel abused." He responded like an ice cube. Without any emotion, let alone concern or compassion, he responded, "Well, if that's the way you feel then you should run away from me as fast as you can because you have it good." Floyd was right. It was an important conversation. That response confirmed that I had to go. There wasn't a marriage to salvage. There wasn't even a friendship. I was living with an enemy.

"Well, then there isn't a marriage to work on. So I guess we need to discuss our living arrangements while we proceed with a divorce," I said.

Our new house had a one bedroom apartment on the first floor (a walkout basement). We had designed it for Danny before he got engaged. And now it was empty. Trying to be conciliatory, I offered to move into the basement and let Dennis have the second and third floors all to himself while we divorced amicably. I thought it was a reasonable plan. I assured him I wouldn't get in his way and just wanted to continue going to school. It would be cost effective. (In hindsight, I don't know why I thought there was any chance he might agree to this.) He said, "No way. Unless you're contributing financially, you cannot live here. You'll have to find someplace else to live or quit school and get a job."

I called Floyd and told him about the conversation. He said, "Dennis has just put you on notice that your welfare is of no concern to him and he does not intend to consider your needs. You need a lawyer looking out for you as soon as possible." I consulted a lawyer that week who advised me not to move out unless Dennis became so intimidating physically that I felt unsafe. He said I would be in a better legal position if I did not willingly give up possession of the house. I told him I was more concerned about my emotional welfare than protecting myself financially, but he did give me some things to think about.

Dennis planned on cutting off all financial support as soon as I left, and I would have to wait on the court to protect me from his wrath. I remembered that during the process of building the house, Dennis boasted to me that he had thousands of dollars in an account I knew nothing about. He had never done anything like that *to my knowledge* before. I didn't understand why he was keeping financial secrets. *Did he think he had to protect himself from me or was he protecting secrets of his own?* I wondered. I had no idea, but this made me feel the need to protect myself. I had two credit cards in my name and had requested secondary cards for Dennis to use. I immediately canceled his cards and paid off the balances. I knew I would need them and did not trust Dennis not to run up debt in my name.

I had paid all of our bills, including utilities, so that everything was current. And I paid off every credit card that I knew about. It was routine for us to pay the balance in full every month, so this was not out of the ordinary. After paying everything off, there was six thousand dollars in our joint checking account. I told my dad that I had nowhere to go, and he was receptive to the idea of me living with him until I could get on my feet. He was also glad I was finally leaving Dennis.

I moved quickly at this point. A new semester was about to start and I was beginning my first year at Lipscomb University. After maintaining a 4.0 GPA for two years at Volunteer State Community College, I won a scholarship to finish my degree at Lipscomb. I was so thankful to be in a position to continue in school in spite of Dennis' threats that I'd have nothing if I left him. I got some help and moved a few things out of my house and into two small bedrooms at my dad's house. I put a bed and dresser in one room and my computer, desk, and exercise bike in the other. The very next day I filed for divorce. I knew when I left that this was finally the end of the road. I was never coming back.

Despite knowing that it was the right decision, a good decision, to end the marriage, I was an emotional wreck. I sat across the desk from my new attorney and cried as I shared details of the marital abuse and how I lived. She came over to where I was sitting, put her arm around me, and comforted me. She had suffered abuse herself and had represented other victims as well. She emphasized how important it was for me to stand up for myself and resist Dennis' attempts to bully and intimidate me. She explained that she could predict his next move without even meeting him. As soon as he knew I had filed for divorce, he would close the bank account and cut me off from any financial support. She said I was within my rights to take every penny of the six-thousand-dollar balance, especially in light of knowing he had money in another account in his name only. I told her my conscience would not allow me to wipe out the bank account, but I felt comfortable taking half of the balance. Out of my three thousand dollars I paid her a fifteen hundred dollar retainer. I knew my dad wouldn't let me starve, and I had credit cards with a zero balance if I needed them.

I knew Dennis would be furious when he was served with the divorce papers, not so much because I was divorcing him but because I was strong enough to state in the paperwork that I was filing for divorce on grounds of emotional abuse. As expected, he was livid when he found out I had taken money out of our account. He had lost some of his power over me. As soon as he received the divorce papers, he closed the account and began making threats. He told Danny, "I will make sure your mother gets nothing if it's the last thing I ever do."

Although a new battle had just begun, the war of the marriage was over. The light at the end of the tunnel was freedom from Dennis. And freedom was now in view.

Chapter 12
FREEDOM

"Passivity is not humility. Fear is not humility. Groveling is not humility. Humility comes out of a deep knowledge that we are loved and held secure. We don't have to prove anything anymore. We have One on our side who is utterly reliable, utterly faithful, utterly for us. This gives us courage to move forward and walk with God in dependence and trust, to move to the rhythms of justice, love and mercy that set us free." —Kim V. Engelmann

THE FALL OF 2002 WAS AN EMOTIONAL ROLLER-coaster, but I was excited about my first semester at Lipscomb University. I felt such a sense of accomplishment for having been awarded an academic scholarship. This particular scholarship was given to only one nontraditional student transferring from a community college each year. And I worked hard for it. It covered two-thirds of my tuition as long as I was a full-time student and maintained a 3.5 GPA. Even though Dennis was making a lot of money, I had been concerned about the expense of a private university. I didn't want my education to be a financial burden. We had recently put Danny through college, and although Dennis was more than happy to pay for our son's education, I knew he would resent paying the expensive tuition for mine. I wasn't even sure he would agree to it when the time came to transfer.

Volunteer State had been an economical alternative. But after two years I needed to transfer to a four-year school in order to finish my degree. I feared Dennis would try to make me feel guilty about the cost of school as a way of deterring me. But if I had a scholarship, I would have earned the opportunity to continue. While I was going through the application process, I wasn't anticipating a divorce at all. I was simply trying to navigate the obstacles Dennis, as my husband, might put in front of me. After I filed for divorce, I realized just how much of a blessing the scholarship was. My fear of Dennis' resistance actually helped me in the end.

I remember a conversation I had with my brother Chris. He was so supportive and always showed an interest in what I was learning. He knew the resistance I was up against. One day he told me he hoped I wouldn't let Dennis pressure me into quitting. He knew I'd worked hard and deserved to finish without feeling guilty. Any time I received encouragement like this, it helped strengthen my resolve. I had been beaten down mentally and emotionally for so long. Dennis mocked me for my lack of drive and ambition, but he always stood in the way of anything that would build my confidence. I was finally seeing clearly that he resented my dedication to school because it built confidence and threatened his power over me. He wanted to control how I felt about myself. He wasn't comfortable with the validation and praise I received from professors and other students. I made the remark to a friend during this time that Dennis wanted to be the center of my universe and that's why he was having a hard time with my focus on school. She replied, "Oh, no. He doesn't want to be the center of your universe. He wants to be the universe."

One of the surprises for me after I left the marriage was finding out how many people recognized that Dennis deliberately held me back. Long after we'd divorced, I had lunch with someone I hadn't seen in years. She was reading my first book, and I asked her if she had been surprised by the divorce. She had been in our home frequently, and I wondered whether or not she had recognized any signs of the abuse. She told me she had two distinct memories of Dennis. First, he always sat in the same spot and expected to be waited on. The other observation was, "You were naturally so bubbly and full of life, but Dennis always seemed to want to suppress your sparkle."

As long as I was living with Dennis and trying to save the marriage, I was frustrated and confused by him. I could never understand the rage or the contempt that came out of him. After I left him, it was like a veil was lifted. As I read books and studied psychology I learned a term that described Dennis' behavior and the way I always felt in response to him. It's called "crazy-making." A person like Dennis often causes others to feel anxious and even downright crazy. No matter how hard you try, you can't avoid triggering the unpredictable flashes of temper and caustic sarcasm. You're always trying to figure out what you did wrong. Although there are occasional rests, you feel like the bout is never really over. You may have to defend yourself at any given moment. You live in anticipation of the next blow. Here I go again using boxing metaphors, but that's how it feels. The bell rings and you know you have to go another round. Then it's back to your lonely corner. Anyone who comes to your emotional rescue and offers validation or reassurance helps prop you back up mentally for the next challenge.

From the first conversation Dennis and I had about divorcing, he insisted I would have to quit school and get a job. He had no intention of contributing anything to my support. He desperately wanted to take school away from me and it was purely out of spitefulness. He refused to give me money. When I asked if he would keep our checking account open with just enough money in it that I could use my debit card for gas, he said, "You have your own credit cards. Use them."

Since Dennis was living alone in 4500 square feet and I was crammed into two tiny bedrooms at my dad's, I felt justified in going back to our house and getting a few additional items to make my time at my dad's more comfortable. One of those items was the TiVo box. I knew he'd refuse to let me have it if I asked, so I just went and got it. He could well afford to replace it, and I had taken so little in comparison to all the luxuries he was still enjoying. When Dennis found out I had been at the house, he acted as if I had robbed him blind. He changed the locks, so if I wanted anything else, I had to ask permission and go into my own home under his supervision. It was the only way he could exert power over me at that point, and he relished doing so at every opportunity.

One day I asked if I could pick up my bread machine and a few other items I had overlooked the day I moved out. He stood over me in the kitchen and watched me the entire time as I packed several boxes of odds and ends. Dennis needed to win every battle. He told me to hurry up, that he had an appointment and needed to go. I told him I could let myself out and lock the door behind me. After all, it was still my house too. Oh, no. That was unacceptable. He informed me that it was his house now, and he was calling the shots. He didn't trust me there alone and added, "You aren't in control of anything now, and you'll have to get used to it." He escorted me to the front porch with my boxes and then locked up the house and left.

Some of the boxes didn't fit in my little car. So I called Cheryl and asked if she would come over in her van and help me transport a few things. To this day, she remembers the painful emotions she felt as she pulled up and saw me sitting alone with my boxes on my own front porch, locked out of the house. At that point, I was still at his mercy. I would have to wait several months for my day in court.

Dennis immediately had a girlfriend the same week I left. (That was who his appointment was with when he locked me out of the house with my boxes.) When I found out her name, I knew a relationship had started *before* I left. They had been playing racquetball together for a long time and Dennis repeatedly had mentioned how attractive she was. I hadn't ever been suspicious of anything inappropriate, but in hindsight it all made sense. One day I was walking through the hallway and heard Dennis answer the phone. I didn't know who was on the other end of the line, but I could tell he was delighted to hear from whoever it was. He talked for a while and when he hung up I asked who he was talking to. He told me it was Ellie. They had had a falling-out on the racquetball court and hadn't talked in a long time. He admitted he'd been a jerk and was afraid he had lost her friendship for good. That's why he was so happy to hear from her. I did not suspect anything beyond friendship at the time. But when I found out that he was romantically involved with her immediately after I left, I realized how naïve I had been.

The first thing I thought about was his accusation that I was cheating on him because I was coming home late and taking baths; he had projected his behavior onto me. And the cold indifference he showed the day I told him I felt abused now made perfect sense. He was going to show me just how quickly and easily I could be replaced. What he didn't realize, though, was how relieved I would feel when I found out he had moved on so quickly. My biggest struggle after leaving had been the fear of God being displeased with me for ending the marriage. Not knowing that Dennis was already involved with someone else, I agonized over being the one to leave. In *Breaking the Chains*, I wrote in more detail about pleading with God to take away my anxiety if I had not displeased Him. His response to my prayer was nothing short of miraculous to me. He covered me with a blanket of His peace almost instantaneously. And I never again battled the tears and overwhelming anxiety I had been suffering with up to that moment. In faith I took hold of my perceived answer that God did not require me to stay in the marriage. But now that I knew Dennis was involved with another woman, I felt completely released from any sense of duty toward him. I actually danced a jig in my dad's kitchen. I felt so free.

The freedom was bittersweet, though. I wouldn't say I was completely happy. The uncertainty of my future was daunting. It was hard to accept failure after spending nearly three decades trying to keep my marriage afloat. I struggled with anxiety and tears nearly every day for a while. And I definitely felt alone at times. But in spite of the disappointment and loneliness, I never once missed Dennis or his company. It was sheer relief to be away from him and know that I would never be his punching bag again.

Two months later, in October, I opened an email from Dennis. He told me he missed "us" and wished I would consider calling off the divorce and come home. He added, "I even miss your long stories." I laughed. It was a sweet email. He told me that he was crying as he wrote it. He said that he realized his priorities were all wrong; that money and a big house were not the important things in life. He said that he'd always believed we would make a great team as grandparents. And he was sorry for mistreating me. He would like the chance to make it up to me and show me that he was sincere. Words like these had always worked in the past, and I'm sure he expected them to work again. The email brought tears to my eyes as I read it, but I knew he hadn't changed. Even the way he expressed himself was revealing to me. He didn't say he missed "me." He said he missed "us." I was an extension of him, not my own person. And I did not miss that.

In my reply email I shared that as I read his words I too was crying. But mine were tears of sadness that it took two full months of separation and my filing for divorce for him to even consider that his priorities had been misplaced, to admit he'd done anything wrong, and to feel a desire to work on the marriage. After twenty-seven years and everything we had been through, his first impulse was to throw me away like garbage. I reminded him that we'd been down this road so many times before and I tried to explain my hopelessness as kindly as I could:

> Every time you've made these promises in the past, I believed you. And every single time you stomped on my heart. I am convinced that the sincere feelings you're expressing right now would not be lasting if I came home. It would be no time at all before you'd be feeling contempt for me again and taking me for granted. And while I believe in your sincerity and I appreciate your heartfelt words, I hope you understand that I just can't trust you with my heart ever again. But I don't want to be your enemy. I sincerely hope we can be friends.

Unfortunately, I did become the enemy again when I said no to him. He thanked me for my honest response and said he didn't want to be enemies either. But his pride immediately took over. He was capable of moments of humility but not sustained humility. The humility he allowed himself to enter into was brief because it was usually a means to an end. If it did not produce the outcome he was looking for, he would feel humiliated and vulnerable. Deep down I knew that he would hate me with a new intensity for turning down his invitation to come home.

It took five months, from August to January, for the first court hearing to determine temporary spousal support. There was a lot of game playing. Dennis delighted in putting me off and refusing support. He'd say, "All you have to do is ask and tell me what you need." But that was never true. He just wanted me to ask so he could enjoy turning me down. All the while, he was making threats about how I wouldn't get anything. After all those years of being at his mercy, I expected him to win and make good on his threats, but my lawyer assured me he wouldn't.

Dennis couldn't stand my attorney. She was a petite woman with a visible impairment (one arm was missing below the elbow), and he had disdain for her simply because she was representing me. He mocked her physical disability, referring to her as my one-armed lawyer. It was disgusting. He thought he was so brilliant, but he wasn't smart enough to realize that remarks like that reflected poorly on him and the kind of man he was. One of his most unattractive traits was his lack of empathy for others.

The day Dennis finally appeared before a judge turned out to be his Waterloo. To my relief the judge was a woman, and I enjoyed that day so much I purchased a transcript of the entire hearing just so I could relive it. He came into court assuming he was going to snow the judge into believing he would never make the kind of money he'd been making after I left. He had essentially stopped working hard and let his income decline intentionally just so that he wouldn't have to pay as much spousal support. His lawyer argued that I had been a real estate agent for years, and I was fully capable of supporting myself. My lawyer had subpoenaed Dennis' financial records, including his credit card statements. And his income might have decreased, but his lavish spending had not. Showing up as regular expenses were spa massages, alcohol, fine dining, even jewelry for his new girlfriend. And he was driving both a Lexus and a newer full-size truck. He said that he needed both vehicles and drove both daily. The judge saw right through him. He looked like a fool to women who were not under his power and control the way I was.

Before the judge made her ruling she explained: "You are trying to convince this court that due to circumstances beyond your control, your income has decreased and you have no expectation that you will be able to produce the level of income you were enjoying at the time of your separation. But your spending does not reflect that expectation."

She awarded me the monthly support I had requested and made it retroactive. He became agitated and started speaking to her directly instead of letting his lawyer do the talking. He told her that if she made him pay that amount, he would not be able to make his house payment and would lose the house in foreclosure. She told him it would be a mistake for him to let that happen. She wasn't buying it. In response to the argument that I was capable of getting a job and supporting myself, she informed him that I had taken school seriously and maintained a 4.0 GPA. I had demonstrated that it wasn't a whim or a hobby. Furthermore, she explained that the court looked favorably on women bettering themselves through education. I had worked hard to earn a scholarship that paid nearly all of my tuition, and she was not going to instruct me to quit school and get a job. She said I was entitled to live in the same lifestyle I was accustomed to after a long marriage in which I had been a homemaker and a stay-at-home mother.

I had not expected such a huge triumph. After all those years of being his victim, I feared being steamrolled by Dennis in the divorce as well. I anticipated the judge would be fooled by him and Dennis would come out the gloating winner. It was obvious that was what Dennis believed too. But it was not meant to be.

Danny and Cheryl were with me in court that day for moral support. Danny had offered to take the stand and testify to his dad's threats if necessary. To my relief it did not come to that. Throughout the divorce, Danny's biggest fear was that I would go back to his dad. It wasn't a matter of putting him in the middle of us. He was a married man now. He was making his own choices. And he had witnessed the abuse. Most kids wish their parents would stay together, but Danny told me that was actually a recurring nightmare of his and the last thing he wanted.

The divorce was contentious and took ten months to finalize because of money, but Dennis and I finally came to an agreement on a settlement. The divorce was official on June 19, 2003. I left the courthouse that day exhilarated and ecstatic. I was finally free!

As it turned out, Dennis wasn't completely finished trying to harass and intimidate me. Though I was physically free of him and eager for emotional distance, he would make further attempts to engage me in conflict.

༄

After being separated for seven months and knowing Dennis had officially moved on, I discovered the world of online dating. I felt conflicted about dating prior to my divorce being final but decided to purchase a subscription to Match.com, telling myself I was just going to make some new friends. I did not expect to meet someone online with whom I would have a serious relationship. I thought of it as a fun diversion until I met the *right* person in *real life*. I bought a year's subscription but kept my profile private. Over the next few months I developed email friendships, talked on the phone, and went out on dates with guys I believed I had "screened" well.

Toward the end of May, just weeks before my divorce was final, I discovered a profile I had never seen. I looked at his picture and his religious preference. I looked to see if he was a non-smoker. I read his comments. I liked everything I read, but the one thing that really sparked my interest was one little sentence, "I think anger is an ugly emotion." Kindness and gentleness were high priorities for me.

John had been in two bad marriages. His first wife became an alcoholic and cheated on him repeatedly. She ultimately died at the age of forty-six as a result of her addiction. They had been divorced for many years, but John had continued trying unsuccessfully to help her for their daughter, Brittany's, sake. He fought for and won custody of Brittany when she was three years old after her mother had taken her to another state and was not caring for her appropriately. He was then a devoted single dad for five years before he remarried. At the time of his remarriage, Brittany was eight years old and what she wanted more than anything was a mother and a family. John believed she would have that with his remarriage. But he says he painfully realized he might have made a mistake within the very first week of living together as a family. Nevertheless, he was determined to honor his vows and try his best to make it work. He truly wanted to have a successful marriage, and the last thing he wanted was another divorce.

John's second marriage was turbulent and stressful. His statement about anger being an ugly emotion stemmed from their constant fighting right from the start. He told me he genuinely loved his wife, but they were never happily married. John explained that they had many challenges, but by far their biggest challenge was the continual friction between his new wife and his daughter, and that he always felt caught in the middle. Trying to be both a supportive spouse and a loving father, he never felt like he succeeded at either because both frequently accused him of being loyal to the other. He felt guilty for the pain and suffering his second marriage had inflicted on his daughter. Although he initially looked forward to having another child with his new wife, he became reluctant and fearful to do so. Finally, his second wife left him and moved into a separate residence, saying she could not live in the same house with Brittany.

John felt like he was being asked to choose between his daughter and his marriage. Brittany was fifteen years old at the time. Obviously, this was an impossible dilemma for John. After more than a year of living separately and leaving the door open for possible reconciliation, she asked for a divorce and he reluctantly complied. In fairness to his ex-wife (whom I know only casually), I'm sure it wasn't an easy road for her either. She was young and had never been a mom or stepmom before. John had a demanding occupation and, while he was an excellent provider, he also worked long hours. (To be honest, his hours were a bit of a challenge for me in the beginning of our life together. I was happier than I had ever been, but I was sometimes lonely and wished we could spend more time together.) John never claimed he was a perfect husband; only that he was faithful, loyal, and tried to do his best.

John wasn't sure he would ever want to be in a relationship again. He wondered if he was incapable of success as a husband. He shared the self-doubts he had wrestled with after we had been married for a while. I was telling him what a wonderful husband he was and he said reflectively, "I always thought I was a pretty good guy, but after having a second wife leave me,

I started to think that maybe I was just a lousy husband. I'm glad you feel otherwise."

A friend had talked John into posting a profile, but like me he was ambivalent about dating. He too thought it would be nice just to find a friend whose company he enjoyed.

After studying John's profile, I sent him an email inviting him to view my profile. He replied right away, and we made plans to meet for dinner that Saturday night. I was nervous. When he walked up to me in the restaurant, I extended my hand, but he gave me a hug instead. We sat and talked for hours that first date. He never glanced at his watch. He wanted to know all about me. I asked about his past, and he told me that he'd been divorced twice. Knowing *nothing* about the details, I remember thinking that I wasn't interested in being anybody's third try. (We have laughed about this many times. John says my expressive face revealed my thoughts.)

When I shared some of the pain of my past, he was so compassionate. Although I didn't feel any romantic chemistry that night, he impressed me as the kind of person I would want in my life, and I enjoyed his sense of humor. On the way home I remember thinking that I had just made a dear friend. The next morning I had a touching email from him. It melted my heart. We started emailing and talking on the phone every day after that.

There was an almost immediate emotional connection between us. Within two weeks of that first date, we both sensed something special in each other. However, we agreed to be strictly friends until I was legally free. John is an honorable, old-fashioned kind of guy. Even when he knew my marriage was essentially over and the delay was purely over financial matters, he didn't want to cross that line even with a kiss. I loved that about him. I didn't think guys like John existed anymore. The day I left court with my freedom, he was the first person I called. I met him at the mall that evening. We ate popcorn for dinner and saw the movie *Bruce Almighty*. I felt like a high school girl again.

I had hoped there would be a Mr. Right for me one day, but I certainly had not expected him to come along so soon. Our relationship was a wonderful surprise. Although I had loved Dennis all the years I'd spent with him, I immediately knew what I felt for John surpassed anything I had ever experienced before. It felt like a fairytale. I realize a lot of relationships start out with that same feeling and then fizzle over time. But I still feel like Cinderella to this day.

We knew within the first two months of dating that we would spend the rest of our lives together. By August we were planning a January wedding. Our only concern was how his daughter Brittany would respond to our plans. We had gotten serious pretty fast and wanted to make sure she had time to warm up to the idea. I wanted her to be comfortable with me and know that I wanted to be a true friend to her, not a rival for her dad's attention or affection. Fortunately, Brittany warmed up to me more quickly than I expected, and she was genuinely happy about our plans. She asked if she could plan the wedding, and her enthusiasm delighted me.

The next week, Brittany suffered an asthma attack and went into cardiac arrest. She managed to press the intercom button in her room and call for her dad to come. He flew up the stairs to her. And then within the next few moments her jaw locked and she stopped breathing. He knew he was losing her. I was in the other room when John screamed "Brittany!" with such panic in his voice that I instinctively knew her life was in jeopardy. I immediately called 911. This all happened so fast and without warning. When the ambulance arrived, I stood outside her bedroom door and prayed as medical personnel worked aggressively but unsuccessfully to revive her.

Just as the ambulance pulled into the emergency room entrance, the paramedics succeeded in restarting her heart. However, by that time her brain had been without oxygen for close to forty minutes. We think the doctors knew what the outcome would be, but they kept her on a respirator for approximately forty-eight hours as they thoroughly tested and observed her before telling us that she had suffered brain death.

As we kept vigil those two days, I told John that I was committed to him, and no matter what happened I would always be by his side. I didn't know if Brittany would need care for the rest of her life or if she wouldn't be coming home at all, but he wouldn't face the outcome alone. I knew God had put me in John's life for a reason. On August 12 we lost her. And on August 15 we buried her.

We did not move up the wedding date, but I never went back to my dad's. I couldn't stand the thought of John being alone in that house. I knew he needed me, and that was the only reason I moved in with him prior to the wedding. In spite of this, Dennis used our living arrangements to his advantage. One afternoon I answered the doorbell and a police officer asked me if I was Shari Bryant. I said I was. He handed me some legal papers and explained that I was being served with a lawsuit. I was shocked and pretty shaken up when I started reading the petition. Dennis was seeking termination of my alimony because I was cohabitating with John. His attorney demanded detailed records of John's personal finances in order to establish that I was well taken care of and had no need of further support from Dennis. He attempted to summons John to a formal deposition. But then he went even further. Adding insult to injury, in Dennis' petition he alleged that John and I had been having an affair while I was still married to him. I was mortified.

John was the most honorable man I had ever met. Marriage vows were sacred to him. There was nothing but friendship between our first meeting and my final court date less than three weeks later. Dennis had claimed to feel compassion for John in the loss of his only child, but then he turned around and used the situation to his financial advantage just three months after her passing. It was deplorable and sickening to me. I felt awful that John had to deal with such ugliness so soon after losing his daughter. I felt responsible because it was my ex-husband harassing him. I shouldn't have been surprised, but I really would not have expected Dennis to stoop so low in his attempts to hurt me.

It was all so unnecessary. John and I were getting married in a few short months and the alimony was about to end anyway. But now Dennis had picked a fight not just with me but with John too. When John came home that evening, he said he didn't care how much it cost. He would hire an attorney to represent me. He would not let Dennis bully me.

The attorney we retained was trying to work the agreement to make Dennis pay alimony even after our marriage. There was one key legal term he focused on. I told him that had never been my expectation. After months of interrogations and responses, my attorney went to the hearing but was shut down by an email Dennis produced in which I had clearly stated my understanding that alimony did not continue upon remarriage. What my lawyer had viewed as a slam-dunk case was ruled partly in Dennis' favor because of my email. My lawyer blamed me and the email for the judge's ruling, but I reminded him that extended alimony was never my expectation.

The money didn't matter that much to me. I just wanted to get on with my life. The "crazy-making" behavior had not ended with the divorce. Out of one side of his mouth, he was telling people he was happy for me and my happiness with John. But at the same time he was plotting ways to harass us. I wondered if Dennis hoped the lawsuit would cause a rift between John and me. He simply lied to the court when he cited an extramarital affair in the legal papers. He knew that wasn't true. He just wanted to upset me any way he could. It was punishment for going on with my life and being happy.

Dennis didn't get out of any rightful alimony as a result of the litigation. But he did cause all of us to spend additional money needlessly. And it would take another four years plus more litigation to finally receive the retirement funds he had offered as part of my divorce settlement. With Dennis nothing was ever easy. He looked for any opportunity to push my buttons and further punish me. He insisted on several occasions after I left him that I would never be as well off financially as I could have been if I had stayed in the marriage. But money was never a motivating factor for me. I would rather scrape by financially and be loved and respected, than have all the money in the world and be emotionally abused. Dennis always expected me to wind up with "some loser" (his exact words) and regret leaving him. I doubt it ever entered his mind that I would wind up being happier than I had ever been. I don't think he imagined me being treated well or appreciated by anyone—because he didn't see me as valuable. If he had, he wouldn't have neglected and abused me all those years. And one thing I know for certain is that he didn't expect me financially to be in a position to fight him legally for my settlement. I believe he was banking on my inability to fight him. He played dirty and often got his way with these kinds of tactics. The games he played made him feel powerful and intellectually superior, but they were frustrating and irritating to me.

There would have been some degree of satisfaction in telling Dennis I didn't need the settlement, and there were times when I entertained the idea out of sheer mental exhaustion. I didn't like the way Dennis was able to toy with me emotionally even after I was married to someone else, and we didn't *need* the settlement. I just wanted to move on and never have to engage with him again. People like Dennis drain you to the point that you are willing to forfeit just about anything to get away from them. But I was stronger at that point and had a strong, resourceful man beside me. John believed that on principle alone Dennis should be compelled to abide by the agreement. I remember John saying to me, "After all the hell that man has put you through, you are going to get your divorce settlement from him no matter how much we have to spend on attorney fees. He should feel lucky he got off with six months of alimony instead of three years. You deserve so much more than your settlement for the twenty-seven years he abused you. And he can play this game if he wants to, but he will not win."

I was in awe that anyone could love and cherish me the way John did. My husband is a gentleman. I have never seen him mistreat or disrespect a single person. And he never looks for a fight, but he also is not intimidated by anyone. And if a fight was what Dennis wanted, that's what he got. John's support encouraged and empowered me to be resolute in standing up for myself even when my emotional energy waned.

John's love was liberating. From the beginning of our relationship, I could be myself with him. He loved and appreciated me for who I was. He didn't find fault with me. He didn't want to change me. And he didn't have ego issues. I've never had to walk on eggshells with him. He listens to me and gives me the freedom to express whatever is on my mind without consequences. He is also quick to apologize if he unintentionally hurts my feelings. And I have never doubted for one moment that I am as important to him as he is to me. I have never felt so safe or secure with anyone in my entire life.

Even though the sparring with Dennis was not quite over, I was no longer at his mercy. I had stopped being his victim. There would be no more cowering, fearing, or enabling. I was free.

Chapter 13
RECOVERING

"The painful events of our past create deep-seated trauma, shame, and cognitive distortions that negatively shape the present until they are exposed and challenged. . . . We cannot put the painful past behind us until we have fully grappled with it." —Steven R. Tracy

THE ONLY RECURRING DREAMS I HAVE EVER HAD ARE nightmares that I am still trapped in my life with Dennis. The details change, but they all have the same theme. I am suffering the abuse that had once been so routine but with the knowledge of what it is like to be in a healthy relationship with a kind, compassionate husband. That's what makes them so much more horrific than when I was experiencing it in real life. In real life I experienced the abuse but didn't know anything else. In my dreams I experience the abuse but know what I am missing. In some of my dreams I simply feel trapped like a prisoner and desperate to escape. In other versions, I am desperately trying to get to John and his love, but I can't get away from Dennis and believe that *God* is making me stay with him. Displeasing God has frequently been a part of these dreams. I agonize over not wanting God to be mad at me. I believe this is a symptom of my "spiritual baggage"—having been raised to believe God required my perfection in order to please Him—in conjunction with the residue of years spent in an abusive marriage. I no longer believe God required me to stay in an abusive marriage.

These dreams are so vivid and so real. A few times I have even yelled in my sleep. John would gently wake me up with reassuring words, and I would feel fantastic relief that I was next to John. I would feel overwhelming thankfulness for him and his love.

These nightmares outlived Dennis, who died in 2011. They have diminished in frequency, but I still occasionally have bad dreams about him. I also still have emotional triggers. Certain words or negative reactions to my requests cause a reflexive, involuntary response. I can control my behavior when these emotions are triggered, but I cannot control the emotional reaction.

For instance, one of the ways Dennis antagonized me was by intentionally picking at me and baiting me until I got worked up. Then he would say in a condescending and belittling tone, "Relax," as if I was overreacting to nothing. It was so calculated most of the time. Only at the very end of the marriage was I able to stop reacting, and that was because I had emotionally shut down and checked out, which isn't healthy. Narcissists need constant engagement and any form of engagement will do, so when I stopped reacting to him, Dennis felt a loss of power over me that was unacceptable to him. It didn't take long for the marriage to crash and burn once I stopped reacting. But for most of the twenty-seven years, I was successfully manipulated this way.

To this day I cannot handle anyone saying to me, "Relax" or "Calm down." Those are fighting words. When I hear them, I have a visceral reaction. My adrenalin pumps. My heart races. It doesn't matter if the words are said in a comforting tone or a humorous tone. Even my adored husband cannot say those words to me without triggering this internal response. And he is kind enough to consciously avoid using those words because he knows how they affect me. I've also explained to others close to me how those words affect me so that they will not misinterpret my reaction if those words are used.

I now have four grandchildren; three adorable grandsons and one beautiful granddaughter. I enjoy spending time with all of them. On one occasion, I had kept my two oldest grandsons overnight and had allowed them to drink some chocolate Ensure that I diluted with milk. I thought it was a great treat. When I told Rebecca about the Ensure, she expressed concern that children probably shouldn't drink the supplement because it was intended for adults. Always seeking her approval as a grandmother, I was afraid my daughter-in-law thought I had done something harmful. I explained how I'd diluted it and was sure it couldn't possibly be harmful. And with the kindest intentions she said, "*Relax*, Grandma Shari." She meant to reassure me that she knew I would never hurt the kids, but I heard Dennis' voice. Every cell in my body became electrically charged with anxiety. I felt hurt and angry even though I knew she hadn't meant it in a condescending way. Unfortunately, we cannot control our feelings, only our actions. I told her that those words were strong emotional triggers. When I explained what those words did to me physically, Danny (who was sitting a few feet away) spoke up and said, "I knew the minute those words came out of her mouth how they made you feel. I had the same internal reaction as you." There are varying degrees of post-traumatic stress, but anyone who has suffered abuse likely suffers from some level of post-traumatic stress. While mine might not be as bad as someone who was kidnapped or raped, it is still very real and intense for me.

Another emotional trigger for me is when I perceive someone suggests I'm doing something wrong with a bad motive. My first impulse is to equate doing and being. I so want to be a good person. I want to have right motives. I want to please God with the way I live my life. And there's nothing wrong with those aspirations. But because of my past, I can slip into the trap of perfectionism. Being flawed is not the equivalent of being bad, except in the mind of a perfectionist and/or a person battling toxic-shame. None of us is perfect. We all make mistakes. Even with the best of intentions, we fall short.

I have shed the conscious belief that I am defective and unlovable (clinically defined as toxic-shame), but occasionally I still contend with a reaction that stems from those long held beliefs. As I was writing the chapters that chronicle my abusive marriage, my emotions were closer to the surface than usual. I'm an emotionally sensitive person by nature, so for me to be emotional means I'm extra sensitive. One day I asked John to do something for me (something he really didn't want to do), and he said, "Oh, don't do that to me." All I heard was him judging me for doing something wrong, something bad, and something selfish. To me, it was an attack on my person. And I started vehemently defending myself as if he had accused me of *being* selfish (even though he didn't). John tried to reason with me but it only fueled my frustration because he didn't understand my reaction (which he couldn't). And he said probably the worst thing he could have said in the moment. In frustration, he said, "I'm not Dennis, Dear." And that didn't set well.

We stopped talking about it for a while until I chilled out. Later, we talked about the trigger point in depth. He said, "I didn't mean it the way you heard it. It was just an expression for me. But when I say something dumb like that, why can't you just smack me on the leg and say, 'Don't be that way' instead of getting upset, and thinking you have to defend yourself?"

It was like a light was turned on for me. It had never occurred to me that I *could* have responded that way. He enabled me to see that I actually *was* reacting to him as though he were

Dennis. "Don't do that to me," heard through my filters was an accusation that I was bad and selfish (like the time I stepped over the newspaper and had my character assassinated by Dennis). That wasn't what John was saying. John has never questioned my heart or attacked my character. But those were words that were frequently spoken to me in judgment and anger for almost thirty years. My feelings and requests were always an imposition, a hassle, or an unwanted demand in my previous marriage. And John's choice of words opened my emotional wounds. In hindsight, it's all very clear to me why I reacted so emotionally. And I was further frustrated that John couldn't *understand* why I was upset. In the moment I thought *I knew* why I was so upset. However, once the initial emotion passed, I was able to see my reaction for what it was. And we were both able to laugh about it. Little reminders like these ever-present triggers make me realize that recovering from years of abuse is a long process. I may have emotional triggers for the rest of my life. But I have taken many more steps forward than steps back.

John and I are extremely compatible, and we genuinely like and respect each other. We have different temperaments and sometimes different priorities, but we share the same values and a deep appreciation of each other. We complement each other and help each other grow both spiritually and relationally because we recognize and admire one another's strengths. There isn't any competition between us. Therefore, we tend to bring out the best in one another. That does not mean, however, that we always agree or see eye to eye.

I have a strong personality (people who love me describe it as passionate) and John is more easygoing. If either of us were inclined to avoid conflict in our marriage, it would be him. But that's not an option for me as I am a born communicator. And any time we disagree, we hear each other out and consider each other's feelings. I can tell John anything without fear of ridicule or rejection. But at the same time I always know he will be honest with me. He doesn't tell me simply what I want to hear. John is not typically emotionally reactive. He is even-tempered to the point that I sometimes wish he'd say, "That's great!" instead of "That's fine." He's not *nearly* as expressive as I am. And there are times I wish *I* could be less opinionated and emotionally expressive, but I have learned to embrace my passion as a trait God intended me to have. When channeled correctly, my passion has served others and me well. I'm grateful John understands and accepts every facet of my personality, including my emotional triggers.

The silver lining of every dark cloud I've ever lived through is found in knowing that God has equipped me through my own suffering to help others with similar wounds. My personal experience, learned knowledge, and four years of intensive counseling have given me insight and wisdom that I can now share with others who feel trapped in their abuse. There is no more instant connection for me than with another woman who has endured an abusive husband. And God has blessed me with many opportunities to be a mentor and friend to women who need the kind of support and understanding I have to offer. I can't begin to describe how rewarding it is for me to know I have helped someone else on their journey. The ability to relate and reach out to others has been a big part of my own recovery.

༄

During my first year of marriage to John, I was invited to participate in a women's study group on marriage. I didn't know any of the women in the group well, and they didn't know me or my background. I viewed the group as an opportunity to make some new friends in my new church community. I assumed most of the women in my group would describe their marriages as ordinary and happy. Sure, they probably experienced some of the routine challenges of being married but no one expressed any deep struggles. If there was anyone else in that room who had experienced the kind of abuse I had, I didn't know it. But often groups of people who don't know each other well don't get to the level where their deepest wounds are.

In the group we read the book *The Excellent Wife* by Martha Peace. The book claims to be biblically based and advocates the concept of submission in a healthy marriage. Some people have a hard time with this idea. But it seems to me that if a husband loves his wife as sacrificially as Jesus loves the church, laying his life down for her, then it is a mutual submission, not just wifely submission. A wife should be submitting to a husband inasmuch as he is following the Lord and honoring his wife. There are plenty of professing Christian men who use the Bible to defend their oppressive and dominating attitude toward their wives. And that reality presented the greatest amount of tension in the study for me. A husband should never use the Bible as a weapon to oppress another person. In *The Emotionally Destructive Relationship* Leslie Vernick explains:

> "When a husband bullies his wife, his behavior does not describe biblical headship, nor is her forced 'submission' characteristic of biblical submission. The correct terms are *coercion, manipulation, intimidation*, or *rape*—and she is the *victim*. Let's make sure we use the right words."

My goal is neither to endorse nor criticize Martha Peace as an author. It just wasn't a book I could wholeheartedly embrace, even though I do believe in biblical submission. I had experienced the opposite ends of the spectrum in my marriages. I had been in a marriage of abuse and exploitation, and now I was in an idyllic marriage where I was loved, valued, respected, honored, cherished, and treated like gold. I was so crazy about John and so filled with appreciation for him that there was virtually nothing I wouldn't gladly do for him. Submission to a man like John was no challenge for me. But as we read and discussed each chapter, I wasn't thinking about John. For one thing, a man like John isn't preoccupied with having a submissive wife. I was being treated as an equal by a man for the first time. Therefore, I was constantly reflecting on Dennis and his abuse. In every directive, I would think about the results *my* efforts to be an "excellent wife" had brought in my abusive marriage. The results were not a more fulfilling or harmonious or God-honoring marriage. The results were more abuse and exploitation. For instance, Martha Peace tells women that their role is to submit to their husband's authority and, "use your energies to glorify him." She explains that a husband is glorified when a wife obeys him and goes on to describe at length the many ways a wife can obey her husband's commands, seek to further his goals, and defer to his will. Later in the book, Peace explains that "Probably the most helpful thing you can do is ask your husband to hold you accountable for showing respect to him. If he agrees, he would, then, point out your disrespectful words, tone or countenance. . . . How willing you are to let your husband help you in this way will reflect your level of maturity and commitment to the Lord Jesus Christ." As I would read passages like those and others, I would think about how Dennis abused and exploited *all* of my sincere attempts to be the kind of wife I was taught to be. Nothing was ever enough to make Dennis feel respected or appreciated. I knew the author was not advocating that women submit to abuse, but after living through it for so long, that was the filter through which I read those passages. And since not all women in an abusive marriage even know they are being abused, it seemed like this kind of book would only reinforce to an abused woman that she must surely be failing if these efforts did not bring about a godly marriage. I felt protective of those women readers and questioned, in my mind, the level of wisdom and understanding (on the subject of abuse) this author actually possessed.

For twenty-seven years I was dominated and controlled by my abusive husband. My legalistic religious upbringing played a distinct role in my enabling the abuse. Despite all my good intentions and strenuous effort, I still felt like I had personally failed. And this is the anguish of many Christian wives who tolerate abuse. Nobody with even a marginally healthy marriage fully understands how devastating this failure is for women like me. We feel the stigma of divorce because we believe in biblical marriage, and books like this tend to reinforce our shame, even though it may not be the author's intent.

It took four years of Christian counseling to convince me that I had been enabling ungodly behavior when I thought I was being the kind of wife God expected. My understanding of marriage was shaped by a legalistic view of Christianity and a heavy emphasis on the wife's role. So it was hard for me to digest the book because I kept thinking about the oppressive religion I grew up under and the abuse of Dennis. I had compassion for the women reading that book who might be struggling with being submissive to their abusive husbands. I was troubled as I kept thinking about women who were in unhealthy or abusive marriages trying to follow these principles. I knew from experience that men like my previous husband would only exploit wives who tried to follow the advice in this book. I had tried for almost twenty-seven years to please God by being "a good wife." Of course I did not do it perfectly, but until I filed for divorce in 2002, I never stopped trying to do the right thing. And my efforts never resulted in a loving or a healthy marriage, let alone a godly marriage. Why did God not honor my efforts? Why did He allow me to be oppressed and abused for so long? I still don't have answers to all my questions, but I know God redeems our efforts, as well as our failures, for His glory if we trust Him. He just doesn't necessarily do it in the ways we often expect. This is a broken world and divorce happens, despite God's original intention for marriage to be between one husband and one wife "till death us do part." Divorce is not the unforgivable sin. Sometimes, despite all their good intentions, Christian authors get it wrong on this subject when they over-emphasize the wife's role in marriage. There are many situations where, despite all the prayer and effort and long-suffering of an abused wife, the abusive man will never change, honor her, or glorify God. In those cases, I now believe with all my heart it is her duty as a Christian *not* to submit to his ungodly behavior.

My emotions ran the gamut during that study. I cried every time I offered a comment. I didn't just get misty. Tears would roll down my cheeks, and sometimes I could hardly get my words out. One of the women in that study—who didn't know me at the time but became a good friend later—told me that I cried so much and so often, she wondered if something was wrong with me. Sometime after the study, I called one of the women from the group. When I told her my name, she didn't remember me. But when I said, "I'm the one who cried all the time," she instantly responded, "Oh yeah! I do remember you!" We both laughed.

After four studies in a row on marriage, I realized that they were keeping me in a state of constant reflection. Some reflection is good, but too much can be a distraction from the present. Although I needed a break from books on marriage, these studies were beneficial in my ongoing recovery. The final step in recovery involves drawing from the valuable life lessons you have learned to help others. And as I shared the contrast between my past and present marriages, I believe I inspired thankfulness and appreciation in some of my new friends for their *imperfect but loving husbands*.

Chapter 14
DISCOVERING KINDNESS

"Kindness and honesty can only be expected from the strong."—Author Unknown

WHAT WOULD IT BE LIKE TO HAVE A HUSBAND WHO was nice to me, I used to wonder. Not today, because I'm married to a kind husband now. I was with a group of friends recently and the subject of remarriage came up. One divorced friend talked about her long list of things she was looking for in a potential mate. A friend who had since remarried after an abusive marriage laughed and said, "I didn't have a list. All I wanted was someone to be nice to me."

"Me too!" I chimed in. We were able to laugh about it because those days were behind us. But in the middle of our cruel years, it wasn't a laughing matter. I remember the bullying and disrespect I was subjected to daily. In his mind, it was my *job* to meet every perceived need and expectation he chose to put on me. Dennis expected to be waited on at all times. He never offered to get anything for me. When we went to a convenience store, he would send me in to get his Big Gulps of Diet Coke. When we went to the yogurt shop, he would wait in the car while I went in to get his treat. He was lazy and demanding. He wouldn't even get up and refill his own drink at a fast food restaurant. When we stayed in a hotel, I was always the one sent out for food, drinks or ice. When we were at home, he sent me out to the store. He rarely offered to go himself. It wasn't that it was so hard on me to do these things for him. In fact, if I had been doing it voluntarily, it would have been an act of kindness on my part. But because he constantly demanded it and reciprocation was so rare, I resented him for it. And if I ever refused his demands, he would punish me by yelling at me and then giving me the silent treatment. He was capable of making life miserable for days over not getting his way in the most trivial situations. He had to win, which meant I had to lose. And it was almost always about winning and being in control for him. His behavior was constant throughout the entire twenty-seven years. It just wasn't worth the grief of trying to stand up to him on little things.

One evening I was having dinner at Outback with my son. Dennis was driving back from a business trip to Atlanta. We were going to arrive home about the same time, so I called his cell phone and asked if I could bring him something from the restaurant where we were eating. He wanted a Blimpie sandwich instead, and he wanted me to go there and get one for him before coming home. (This was during the time I had been in counseling and learning to stand up for myself.) Since the Blimpie was out of my way but was on his way home, I asked if he would *mind* picking it up for himself. Well, his temper flared (simply because I asked) and we wound up in a fight. Danny rolled his eyes and said, "It must be hard being married to a two-year-old." At the end of the tense phone conversation, Danny reminded me, "You shouldn't have called to offer him *anything*."

My counselor told me if I wanted a healthier, more respectful relationship, I needed to stop giving in to Dennis' demands. It's hard to work up the courage to set boundaries with a narcissist. It's easier to give them their way, but it's destructive to them and to the relationship. And it sets a bad example for children. I was afraid of Dennis. Not so much physically, but he was so mean and so emotionally punishing when I dared to challenge him. He had so much anger inside him. I lived in anticipation of his wrath. I feared the explosions of temper and hateful words. I feared doors slamming and pictures falling and the look in his eyes when enraged. I hated being belittled and degraded. I dreaded being given the silent treatment. And that's how I learned the art of walking on eggshells. It became second nature to me.

Closer to the end of the marriage, I did stand up to Dennis more. We were in California visiting some friends. While we were out and about, he decided he wanted a frozen yogurt. He pulled into the parking lot, picked up a newspaper off the back seat to read and told me what he wanted, assuming I would be fetching his yogurt for him as usual. I carefully weighed the consequences of refusing him and chose to be brave that day. I told him I didn't want a yogurt and asked if he'd go in for himself. He refused. I carefully stated that I didn't mind going in for him some of the time, but it would be nice if he would occasionally offer to go in himself. He reminded me that I didn't work to earn the living, and he expected me to do things for him. He was getting irritated, but I was mentally prepared to stand my ground. It wasn't about the yogurt. It was about not being treated like his slave. It was about never having the option to say no to his demands and always being taken for granted. We argued back and forth for several minutes, but I did not back down. I wasn't going in this time, even if he got mad and pouted. And sure enough, he blew up. He wasn't willing to go in himself, so he skipped the yogurt. We drove back to our friends' home, and he spent the rest of the afternoon and evening alone in their guest room watching television. I was humiliated by his ridiculous behavior. I told my friend that we'd gotten into a fight and Dennis was not coming out because he was mad and pouting. I tried to blow it off, but I wasn't sure I had chosen the right occasion to stand my ground. An abused woman always doubts herself and wonders if she is to blame for her circumstances.

⁂

Dennis was always so into himself and what he wanted to be doing. It was rare for him to ever offer to help around the house or with any sort of cleaning, packing, or entertaining. It was rare, but I remember one occasion I was helping to give a bridal shower for Rebecca next door at my sister-in-law's house on a Saturday morning. I had done some cooking and baking and had numerous items to carry over. I was going to have to make several trips, but I didn't even consider asking Dennis for help. I didn't want to have any unpleasantness that day. I don't know what inspired him that morning, but he asked if I would like any help. I was so thankful that I cried. I thanked him over and over and told him how much I appreciated him offering to help me. By my reaction, you would have thought he'd given me a ten carat diamond. But that was how much even a little bit of kindness from him meant to me. Unfortunately it was just an isolated event, too little too late.

A divorced friend of mine recently told me how when on a camping trip with friends she was overwhelmed when she received help from some of the men. She wrote me an email explaining: "This weekend was mind-blowing. Completely and totally. I have never had so much energetic, cheerful help ever in my whole life. And not a single man made any comments about me not being adequate or being a burden or why did I go or anything of the sort." When I read her comments, I completely understood why that was mind-blowing for her. Dennis had told me so many times that because I didn't earn income I was "dead weight" in our marriage. My mind instantly went back to that one *big* morning toward the end of our marriage when Dennis had shown me that random kindness out of the blue. It was so unexpected and I was so grateful. I couldn't believe how good it felt. The average woman wouldn't comprehend this level of gratitude for mere common courtesy. But my guess is that the majority of battered and abused women can relate. A little kindness makes us feel like people instead of tables. And in these kinds of relationships, the person being dominated rarely experiences consideration.

Narcissistic people do not have empathy for the feelings of others. Everything is always about them. Of course Dennis was capable of offering gentlemanly help but only if he felt like it (which was rare), and it could never be anticipated or relied upon. That would be perceived by him as an expectation or a demand. Nobody had the right to expect anything of him in his mind. He would tell me when he was lashing out, "You don't appreciate what you have. I am only as good as the last thing I did for you." It was actually the complete opposite. I existed for his use and to reflect his image to others in a positive way. I had no value to him apart from meeting his needs, satisfying his demands and feeding his narcissistic supply. I tried to communicate this in our last attempts at counseling. He acknowledged his demanding behavior and promised to change, but it was only to win me back. He reverted to the same patterns of behavior almost immediately.

Dennis was a troubled and complex person who was difficult to live with. But I accepted him that way. I constantly tried to focus on the positives. I had no illusions of him becoming the man of my dreams or our marriage blossoming into something emotionally fulfilling. If he would have just been nicer to me, I would have been willing to settle for that, but I could never fathom how it could be so hard for anyone to simply be kind.

In *Why Does He Do That?* Lundy Bancroft explains that "Almost no abuser is mean or frightening all the time. At least occasionally he is loving, gentle, and humorous and perhaps even capable of compassion and empathy. This intermittent, and usually unpredictable, kindness is critical to forming traumatic attachments. When a person, male or female, has suffered harsh, painful treatment over an extended period of time, he or she naturally feels a flood of love and gratitude toward anyone who brings relief, like the surge of affection one might feel for the hand that offers a glass of water on a scorching day. But in situations of abuse, *the rescuer and the tormentor are the very same person*" (emphasis added).

∽

The first year I was married to John, I could not get over how consistently considerate and kind he was to me. I felt guilty when he offered to go to the store for me or insisted on doing the dishes after dinner. I almost felt like I was taking advantage of him to let him do these things. I felt so pampered and spoiled. I remembered all the times I had fantasized about what it would be like to have a kind husband. And now I knew. To quote my friend, it was "mind-blowing" amazing.

John consistently helps me and does things for me that quite honestly could be expected of me since I am not working. He doesn't expect things to be done for him. And he doesn't even call my attention to anything he's done. He waits for me to notice. That is just who he is. He takes care of things without expecting any praise. But I am constantly expressing my appreciation and I know he enjoys being appreciated. It shows.

One of the best compliments he has ever given me was during our first year of marriage. Just as I was overwhelmed with his consideration and kindness, he was overwhelmed with my appreciation for him. He had never felt appreciated. One day when I was expressing how much his thoughtfulness meant to me, he said, "All the little things I do around the house are things I have always done. It was just expected of me or I had to as a single dad without help. But you are always so appreciative. I enjoy doing things for you. I have never felt so *worth something* as I have since we have been together."

John is a talented and successful man. He is highly respected and loved by the people who know him personally and professionally. I don't know a single person who doesn't like him, so I was surprised to hear him say that. He treats everyone with kindness and respect. And he has accomplished so much, but it was my love and appreciation that made him feel worth something. Not only did his comment make me feel like a million dollars, it reminded me of how much we all need to feel appreciated by the people we love, even someone like John who never seeks attention or applause for being a good guy. Many compliments later, I still look back on that one as my favorite.

I will never take my husband for granted. It's a terrible mistake that so many people make in relationships. One of the positive things to come out of my many years in an abusive marriage is the constant awareness of my blessings today. I would not appreciate John the way I do if being married to John was all I knew. We are both absolutely certain that if we had married each other first, there never would have been a second marriage for either of us. But we are equally certain that we appreciate each other so much more as a result of our past struggles and the pain we experienced before finding each other.

Kindness and mutual respect are important ingredients in a successful relationship. Studies have shown contempt as a strong indicator that a marriage will end in divorce. Signs of contempt include insults, mockery, hostile humor, negative body language (like eye rolling and sneering), condescending words, and dismissive belittling. Frequent contempt conveys that the person being abused is unworthy of the abuser's respect.

In my particular situation, the contempt could even be veiled in an offhanded compliment. I remember sitting in the car with Dennis in front of a business office one day. We had arrived for a closing and were gathering the paperwork before going inside. While we were sitting there, an overweight woman walked in front of our vehicle and Dennis (being at least a hundred pounds overweight himself) said to me: "I'm glad you have taken care of yourself and stayed thin. I don't think I could be attracted to a heavy woman." He may have been trying to compliment me, but it felt like a warning. And it was offensive. *His* weight wasn't an issue, but he could never find a *woman* with a weight problem attractive. He had no compassion or empathy, and I actually felt protective of the woman walking past us, who had no clue she had become an object of contempt for my husband. He viewed all women as objects unworthy of his respect as human beings. What he appreciated about me was completely superficial and ultimately all about him. I wanted to point out his hypocrisy and arrogance. I wanted to express how offensive his remark was. But I kept my thoughts private and just smiled. A big fight just before the closing would have been inconvenient. It's not like he would have acknowledged my feelings anyway, and perhaps I was feeling some contempt of my own. I loved him, but I did not like him. Truth is I don't like cruel people.

The Bible tells us: "Love your enemies, do good to those who hate you, bless those who curse you, pray for those who mistreat you. If someone slaps you on one cheek, turn to them the other also. If someone takes your coat, do not withhold your shirt from them. Give to everyone who asks you, and if anyone takes what belongs to you, do not demand it back. Do to others as you would have them do to you" (Luke 6:27-31 NIV). In Proverbs 15:1, we are told that "a gentle answer turns away wrath, but a harsh word stirs up anger." I heard these passages quoted frequently throughout my life. And I try to follow these biblical principles to this day. Life with Dennis did not succeed in souring me on the idea of returning good for evil. But it's important for victims of abuse to realize that there is a difference between doing good to those who harm you and enabling ungodly behavior. A narcissistic abuser in all probability will continue to exploit and abuse you in response to your attempts at kindness and goodness. It's also important to remember that doing good may include consequences for wrong. I struggled to understand what God expected of me—and what He didn't—for so many years. Most Christian books on marriage do not address the plight of an abused woman. That's why a good Christian counselor was essential for me in figuring out where that fine line of suffering long in love ended and enabling ungodly behavior began.

I like how Kim V. Engelmann puts it in *Running in Circles: How False Spirituality Traps Us in Unhealthy Relationships*. "If we assume that all suffering is constructive and fail to discern that we are in a self-destructive cycle, we risk missing out on God's plan to give us a 'future with hope' (Jeremiah 29:11)—a plan that takes us somewhere. Again, Jesus didn't succumb to every kind of suffering."

Chapter 15
FORGIVENESS

"My growth has meant pain. The potter's wheel has involved a great deal of tears, prayer and psychotherapy, along with the hard work of forgiveness and a deep resolve to endure so that my shattered life could be 'reset' and I could heal completely." –Kim V. Engelmann

"To be a Christian means to forgive the inexcusable because God has forgiven the inexcusable in you." —C. S. Lewis

FORGIVENESS IS A CHOICE THAT I'VE HAD TO MAKE repeatedly. It isn't a once and done deal. I have sometimes had to fight hard not to harbor animosity toward Dennis. I won't deny that there were times when I felt the desire to inflict the same pain on him that he inflicted on me and others I loved, I just tried not to give in to those feelings. Because we had a son together, and later grandchildren, we had to be together on numerous occasions for family events, which meant I had to put up with Dennis for years after the marriage ended. At family gatherings Dennis seemed to make an effort to be friendly, and I was genuinely happy that Danny was on better terms with his father for a while.

One of the issues I had to put up with was Dennis dragging out the financial settlement for years after the divorce was finalized. I must confess that I resented his lavishing money on Danny, trying to look like a big shot and a hero to others, all the while refusing to surrender the retirement account in compliance with our settlement agreement. I wanted Danny to have the things his dad gave him, but it was still painful because it was a continual reminder of how Dennis was still trying to control me. I'm sure he enjoyed putting me off and thought if he procrastinated long enough, I might just get tired of the hassle. But I was determined not to reward his behavior by giving in to what he wanted. And John backed me up. He was adamant about legally compelling Dennis to fulfill his rightful obligation to me.

Ultimately, when my lawyer petitioned the court to give Dennis a deadline in late 2007, instructing him to either surrender the account or face a court appearance, Dennis finally complied and the matter was resolved through arbitration. It took four years after the divorce was final for me to get my settlement. Even though he could have resolved the matter at any time to put the unpleasantness behind us, he needlessly drug it out just to be difficult. But at that point I was relieved that I was finally done with him legally.

After the last legal matter was resolved, it was easier for me to see Dennis. It was the beginning of a more cordial relationship. There were baptisms and birthday parties and preschool programs. John and I bumped into Dennis and his date at the Tennessee Performing Arts Center one night. I had gone to the ladies room before the performance and left John waiting for me. When I came out, John was standing there talking to Dennis and a woman I didn't know. We exchanged a few friendly words before going to our seats. We ran into each other at concerts a couple of other times, and Dennis always seemed a little nervous. Several times when he extended his hand, I noticed that it was shaking slightly. I thought he was just uneasy around us. I didn't know at the time that he'd developed a dependence on alcohol.

The last time John and I saw Dennis was in December of 2009. We went to see our oldest two grandsons in their Christmas program. Dennis seemed to get a kick out of introducing me to his newest girlfriend because she shared both my first and my middle names. She seemed uncomfortable during the introduction, which was a bit awkward. Dennis was shakier than usual, and I remember thinking that he looked bad.

One day in early 2010, I was volunteering in the administrative office of my church when my cell phone rang. I recognized Dennis' phone number. We had not had a phone conversation in years, and I couldn't imagine why he was calling me. For a moment, I considered letting it go to voice mail, but I didn't want the obligation of returning his call so I picked up. He told me that he had struggled with a serious drinking problem since our divorce, and he was in a twelve-step program. He was rereading my book, *Breaking the Chains*. I never mentioned his abuse in that book, but I touched on some minor issues we'd had leading up to our divorce. While reading the chapter in which I described how I'd felt while trying to juggle school and his resentment, he saw how he'd made me feel for the first time. He said, "I had no idea you felt that way. And even though I've already apologized in a more general way for treating you badly in the past, I just felt like I owed you a specific apology for that period of time." I wanted to say *Of course you had no idea how I felt. It wasn't because I didn't try to tell you. You just never cared about anyone's feelings other than your own.* However, I wanted a good relationship for the kids' sake, so I just thanked him for his apology and told him that, even though it wasn't necessary, I appreciated it. We ended up having a nice conversation. And I explained how I had tried to write as little about him as possible in the book because I didn't want to hurt him.

"Oh, we both know all the things you could have written but didn't. And I want you to know I appreciate that," he said. I told him I had no animosity toward him and truly wanted the best for him. I was glad we were finally friends. And he said he was too. It was such a positive conversation. It was a conversation he should have felt good about. But I learned later that within two weeks of that conversation, he told Danny he regretted the apology and shouldn't have called me. Pride always won out in the end with Dennis. He wasn't growing as a person or changing in a positive way as I'd hoped, and that made me feel sad, not mad.

The last year and a half that Dennis lived was a self-destructive downward spiral.

In August of 2011, John and I were away on a business trip. John had found a Honda dealership in West Virginia that he was interested in buying, and he wanted me to see the area because my feelings about moving were a major factor in the decision. My cell phone rang just as John and I were about to leave our hotel room. It was Danny. He called to tell me his dad was dead. I had always thought Dennis might die young, but I still was stunned as Danny told me what happened. He had fallen and hit his head on the bathtub. He had died as a result of a fatal head wound. And death had come quickly, according to the coroner. Dennis lived alone and it was uncertain how long he'd been dead when he was found. Weeks later, the toxicology report stated that Dennis had suffered a heart attack resulting from hypertensive heart disease. He had suffered from high blood pressure his entire adult life. And he had abused his body for many years. He had not been intoxicated at the time of his death, causing the fall. But certainly the heavy drinking had contributed to his heart disease.

John and I attended Dennis' memorial service to support Danny and his family. We were at the church when Danny and the kids pulled up. We walked out to the front steps, and our oldest grandson came running toward us with outstretched arms. "Poppy John! Poppy John!" he exclaimed. I felt so thankful that God had put John in all our lives. I also could not help but think about how many blessings Dennis had forfeited by gripping his false pride and sense of entitlement so tightly. I am thankful I was spared from sharing the last nine years of his life. I can't imagine how much harder my life might have become had I stayed. In the end, the only life he destroyed was his own. I have truly forgiven him.

The Bible tells us to forgive because we are forgiven. And I take that admonition seriously. However, as Dr. Tracy explains in *Mending the Soul*, "Careful examination of the Bible's teaching on forgiveness reveals very different kinds of forgiveness described within its pages." Dr. Tracy lists three types of forgiveness "that must be distinguished if we are to do justice to the Bible's teaching." Those three categories are judicial forgiveness, psychological forgiveness, and relational forgiveness. Only God can extend judicial forgiveness. Psychological forgiveness "involves letting go of hatred and personal revenge . . . extending grace to the offender." And finally there is relational forgiveness, "the restoration of relationship . . . synonymous with reconciliation." Dr. Tracy states that even though it is the desired goal, "many abusers cannot be given relational forgiveness, for they refuse to do the painful work of repentance." But, as Christians, we can offer psychological forgiveness without necessarily extending relational forgiveness. *I want to make clear that psychological forgiveness is the type of forgiveness I am emphasizing as healing in this book.* Relational forgiveness offered too quickly, trivially, or without genuine repentance and earned trust, "is unhealthy both for the abuse victim and the perpetrator, for it inevitably involves excusing or minimizing sin" according to Dr. Tracy. (I highly recommend reading his entire book for a fuller understanding of biblical forgiveness as it relates specifically to abuse.)

I am not a biblical scholar or a professional psychologist, but for me there is also a difference between willing myself to forgive as an act of sheer obedience and the forgiveness that flows freely from a compassionate heart. That is the heart I want to cultivate. I believe I was empowered to freely forgive Dennis by the genuine compassion I felt for him. I *feel* forgiveness for Dennis in my heart. He was a tortured person. That doesn't mean that I condone his behavior or his choices in life. I am not apologizing for him or excusing his actions. He was the meanest person I have ever known. And every time I saw him post-divorce, I silently thanked God for rescuing me from his cruelty. But I never lost sight of his humanity. Somewhere his life went horribly off track. And out of his misery, he inflicted misery on others. He was his own worst enemy, and I'm thankful I could always feel compassion for him as a victim of himself.

More important than what I went through is how I came through it. I not only survived his abuse, I rose above it. I am stronger and wiser than I would have been without those painful experiences. I also have an ability to empathize with and relate to others that I never could have developed without my own struggles and suffering. I value so highly the lessons I have learned through suffering that I have become genuinely thankful for the painful experiences themselves.

Am I glad the abuse is behind me? Oh, yes! More thankful than I can ever describe! However, I don't see any of my past as an unnecessary part of my journey. I believe God had a plan for my life that included suffering. But more important than that is the reality that His plan included redemption! I was not destroyed by Dennis.

There is a Scripture that says God will "repay you for the years the locust have eaten" (Joel 2:25). When people say "God bless you" to me, I like to say, "Oh, He has!" I am living an abundant life of redemption and restoration. God used all of my life's experiences for my good. Though it wasn't always apparent to me in the middle of my trials, I believed in and clung to the promise of Romans 8:28 (that He is working all things for my good), and my faith was rewarded.

I have often been told by friends that I deserve the life I have today and that John is my reward for the way I endured my past life. But if there is a reward involved, I believe it is my faith that has been rewarded, not my performance. My performance was inconsistent and certainly not always exemplary. I recognize the life I enjoy today is a demonstration of God's love, mercy, and grace more than a reward for anything I have done. I have no desire to give myself credit for earning the goodness of God. I recoil from the idea that I have earned any of my blessings or that He chose me because of some goodness He saw in my heart. And that is because I have come to a fuller understanding of God's grace.

I have always been acutely aware that there is so much more intense suffering in this world than what I have experienced. I have never known poverty or hunger or the struggle for survival that so many others have faced. So I want to keep my suffering in perspective. Compared to many people in this world, I have lived a blessed life from the day I was born. My worst day might be the equivalent of someone else's best day. Reminding myself of that during difficult times has helped me not to sink into despair.

I did not have a spiritually healthy understanding of God during the years I spent in an abusive marriage. I did not understand the Gospel the way I do today. I was taught I had to be perfect to go to heaven. I was works-oriented in my thinking. I believed I had to prove myself to God on a daily basis, that He was never satisfied with me because I made so many mistakes. But it was perhaps even more the people around me (Dennis, my family, Brother and Sister Mears, judgmental people in our church) to whom I felt I had to prove myself. I was desperate for approval and affirmation. It is no wonder that Dennis was able to successfully manipulate me through my desire to please.

It took spiritual de-programming for me to even entertain the idea that God might *not* expect me to suffer marital abuse for the rest of my life. I never dreamed that He might rescue me. But had I not endured Dennis' abuse and wrestled with my role in it, I would not have my testimony or be equipped to help others on their journeys. It is a privilege and an honor for me to have the opportunity to inspire and offer hope by sharing my story of redemption.

Recently, I heard a sermon by Dr. Tim Keller, pastor of Redeemer Church in New York City, in which he eloquently described how our greatest joys are birthed out of suffering. It resonated deeply within me because I knew exactly what he was describing. I was given a gift. And the gift was wrapped in pain. Like the delivery of a baby, my pain brought forth profound joy. And the gift was not only for me. It's a gift I can share with others. It's my overcoming testimony.

On the other hand, while constantly trying to avoid being hurt by others, Dennis robbed himself of so many blessings he might have enjoyed in this life. He took a hatchet to his own life. He continuously erected walls to protect himself from vulnerability. And he died in isolation within the very walls he built. He alienated the people who loved him the most.

There are lessons to be learned from his choices. But those lessons cannot be learned by hating Dennis or objectifying him. To objectify someone is to make them an object (often an object of contempt) rather than seeing them as a human being. When we depersonalize and vilify, we stop seeing our common humanity. Dennis was a multi-faceted person. I have no desire to make him the personification of evil with this book. I don't want you to hate him. I want you to feel compassion for him and others like him. And the most important reason for you to develop compassion is because compassion is the road to forgiveness and also the road to freedom from remaining a victim.

Forgiveness does not imply relationship. Forgiveness does not represent a wink or a nod at unacceptable behavior. It is not a seal of approval on injustice. Forgiveness is releasing someone from owing you for their wrong. We forfeit personal retribution, not justice. We do let it go. But we don't let it go into thin air. We release it to God, recognizing that only He is the all-knowing, all-seeing Judge who will right all wrongs.

I don't hope for Dennis to receive eternal punishment for his wrongs. Life punished him severely with the consequences of his own choices. I lived with him for many years, and I know he hated himself. His treatment of others was a reflection of self-loathing. He projected that onto others. Much of the deplorable behavior exhibited in Dennis and people like him results from shame. You might not always be able to recognize it because narcissists overcompensate for their feelings of inadequacy with arrogance, entitlement and an air of superiority. But narcissists are in reality the most insecure people in the world. It is their neediness that compels them to push you away rather than risk your rejection. Vulnerability makes them feel weak. And their self-esteem is so low that they have to constantly put others down to feel better about themselves. They are driven to compare themselves and compete with others. They are jealous of the successes of others. The slightest criticism is perceived as an attack. And they are often hypercritical of others. They are unable to accept God's grace; therefore they cannot extend God's grace. Shame compels them to blame others for their own failures. Shame often results in addiction and compulsive behaviors. And recovery is made more challenging by the fact that people who cannot engage in healthy reflection and introspection hide not only from others but from themselves. They are desperate to create a false self-image because it protects them from their sense of inadequacy. They live in complete denial of who they are and how they impact people close to them. It's such a sad life. I don't want to be in close relationship with the persons I've just described. But how could I not feel some degree of compassion for their torment and misery?

I recognized there were many facets to Dennis' personality and behavior years before I left him. I experienced being the victim of his narcissism long before I read about it or had it defined for me psychologically. I had accepted that Dennis was shallow and that I would never experience the deep emotional connection with him that some husbands and wives enjoy in marriage. I accepted that as a consequence of marrying at the age of sixteen, before I had even the slightest idea what to look for in a partner. And I was willing to stay in a marriage that held out little if any hope for fulfillment. I was committed to doing everything within my power to make my marriage succeed. I felt like I might be the only person in the world who really understood Dennis and why he behaved the way he did. But ultimately I realized that I was facilitating his behavior, not helping him be a better person. And with the perspective of today, I am less certain that I knew or understood him as well as I thought I did. It always amazes Danny when *any* new information still surprises me about his dad. But my first reaction is still shock and disbelief when I learn of something I never knew (like his lies about my dad).

I remember worrying about Dennis after I left and wondering what would happen to him the next time deep depression struck. During one of my counseling sessions following the separation, I told Floyd that even though I couldn't be married to him anymore, I still loved Dennis. Floyd said, "You feel responsible for Dennis the way a mother feels responsible for her child. What you feel is not the love of a wife for her husband." I understood the distinction he was making at the time. But I didn't grasp the magnitude of his words until I experienced a real marriage with John. My life with Dennis was the only husband/wife relationship I'd ever known. So at the time I truly didn't know what the love Floyd was describing felt like. But now I do.

After John came into my life and became my husband, I realized that I had never before experienced what I felt for him. I finally had a tangible understanding of this distinction rather than recognizing it as a concept. I had never known the respect and admiration for a husband that a woman feels in response to being cherished and lovingly held dear.

I consider *Mending the Soul* by Steven R. Tracy to be the best book I have ever read on the subject of biblical healing. Dr. Tracy emphasizes the power of healthy relationships to heal. "Abuse isolates victims. The good news is that healthy relationships have tremendous power to nurture the soul and heal the wounds of abuse," Tracy writes. John has a knack for fixing things, and he occasionally says, "I can fix anything but a broken heart and the crack of dawn." I always correct him by saying, "I don't know about the crack of dawn, but you fixed *my* broken heart." Of course he didn't really "fix" me. No human being can do that for us. But my relationship with John has unleashed tremendous healing power for me. John does not question my heart or my motives. He reminds me that I don't have to please everyone or compromise my convictions to make people happy. He stands up for me when I am misjudged, and he always emphasizes that he knows my heart and my good intentions. Even when I'm in the wrong, he never tries to make me feel like a bad person with bad motives. That might not seem like such a big thing to someone who hasn't been abused. But to me, it's huge. I never feel like I have something to prove to John.

Forgiveness is one of the greatest gifts we can receive in this life. It is also a gift we can give to others. I think an important thing to remember is that forgiveness is never deserved. Not when we give *or* when we receive it. I do not believe God wants us to continue in abusive relationships or embrace avoidable suffering indefinitely. I believe there are harmful, destructive relationships it is God's will for us to walk away from. But I want to extend God's grace and forgiveness to those who have hurt and abused me because God has extended grace and forgiveness to me. I want to overcome evil with good.

Chapter 16
REFLECTION

"In the pages of Scripture, authentic strength—of the sort that wins battles, overcomes impossible odds, and takes on overwhelming opposition—walks hand in hand with weakness." —Joni Eareckson Tada

As I reflect back on my years of abuse and my own unhealthy responses that helped to perpetuate the abuse from my first husband, I realize that I still struggle at times with some of my old patterns of behavior. I still thrive on approval and affirmation. I sometimes like to please people over doing what is best for them. But I have gained a lot of perspective on my misplaced priorities. One of the books that has helped me the most in this area is *When People are Big and God is Small* by Edward Welch. In it Welch shares some of the most common reasons we are controlled by other people. "They can reject, ridicule, or despise us (rejection-fear). . . . They ignore us. They don't like us. They aren't pleased with us. They withhold the acceptance, love, or significance we want from them. As a result, we feel worthless."

I wish I could tell you that I don't ever battle those worthless feelings anymore when someone disapproves of me or rejects me. Seeing this in myself hasn't cured me. But I have come a long way. I live in the tension of recognizing it and resisting it. But my strongest motivation isn't an aversion to being a doormat. I'm motivated by a desire to love unselfishly, the way Jesus loves me as opposed to loving selfishly; to have my needs met in return. I want to value relationships above pride. I want to be humble and willing to admit when I'm wrong and quick to ask forgiveness when I've hurt someone, even unintentionally. But I don't want to value someone's positive feelings toward me so highly that I grovel for their love or acceptance. That makes them an idol. It's common for victims of abuse to have rejection issues. And I've had to work at overcoming mine. But I have learned that fearing people, their disapproval and rejection, will actually prevent me from loving them unselfishly because I can't risk losing their affection. When we love others unselfishly, we are able to confront them in love without the fear of their rejection.

A friend once told me that she was proud of herself for refusing to continue being abused by her ex-husband but noticed that she was continuing to be a doormat for other people in her life. She had learned to ignore healthy boundaries so well that she had become everyone's doormat, not just her ex-husband's. And fear of unwanted conflict was standing in the way of her ability to assert herself or establish healthier boundaries with others in her life.

I wish I had a simple "how-to" manual to offer when asked "How can I stop doing this?" There was a long process of self-discovery for me before I could begin to change my behavior. I had to learn how to determine what *my* true motives were in many different scenarios. *What was I gaining or avoiding by not enforcing healthy boundaries?* Abusive people will continually tread on you if you let them. Every decision to overlook and accommodate a violation of your boundaries sends a message. You are giving your consent to being mistreated and abused. Not every person who crosses a boundary will do so in an abusive way. But the narcissists in your life will push you further and further with their demands . . . because they can.

Sometimes it's easier to take someone's lack of consideration in stride rather than to risk rocking the boat. We choose our battles in life. But when you find yourself continually choosing not to rock the boat with the same person, all the while trying to stifle feelings of resentment, know that you are not on the path to a healthy relationship with that person. If a healthy relationship is the goal, you have to get on a different path. The path of enabling does not lead to mutual respect. It leads to more abuse. And it was a big turning point for me when I grasped that I am not loving or helping the abusive person by enabling them. They need to be confronted in love. Their behavior will ultimately sabotage *all* of their relationships.

I am especially sensitive to narcissistic behavior now. The red flags pop up quickly for me. Often people don't realize how much they reveal about themselves by their casual remarks in normal conversation. When you've lived with a narcissist and suffered their crazy behavior, you develop radar for other narcissists. I try to avoid these people as much as possible. But if the narcissist in your life is someone you cannot possibly avoid (a family member or coworker), you will have to learn to navigate this relationship. *Why is it Always About You?* by Sandy Hotchkiss is a helpful book on dealing with the narcissists in your life. It was one of the first books I read that helped me understand the constant chaos I lived in.

I have come so far and have healed so much, but I think you should know I still struggle with a few residual effects, even ten years down the road from my abuse. Don't expect to be healed completely immediately. I am reminded that abuse was part of my journey in the way I react to something. Sometimes I still will read between the lines of a comment, perceiving an attack that may not actually be there. I anticipate rejection when there is no threat. I have a tendency to be hard on myself when I make a mistake or say something I regret. But all of these residual effects are diminishing over time. I continue to heal and grow.

It's good to be sensitive to the feelings of others. However, I still tend to over-scrutinize my words, frequently doubting myself and wondering if I could have said something better or differently. I know I developed this compulsive obsession from all the years of having my words twisted and thrown back at me. I frequently over-explain myself and find it painful to be misunderstood. I'm working on that. I have to remind myself that always being fully understood isn't a realistic goal. People are going to misunderstand us. We will all be misjudged by someone. And most of all I have realized finally that I don't owe everyone an explanation for being who I am.

The first year John and I were married I remember going into one of my long explanations. I don't remember why, but I feared he would misunderstand my intent about something. He had a sympathetic look on his face as he interrupted me and said, "You do not have to constantly explain yourself to me. I know your heart." Those were such soothing, healing words to my damaged soul. "I know your heart."

My wish for every survivor of abuse is a healing relationship. It may happen sooner or later, but just know that struggles are a part of life. You will overcome some of your struggles, only to have them be replaced by new ones. But don't be discouraged by an occasional reminder of the abuse you've suffered. Don't think it's a sign you haven't healed as much as you thought you had or hoped you would. Instead, let those occasional reminders focus your attention on how far you've come. And be grateful.

It's been over a decade since I escaped my abusive marriage. I am not stuck in constant reflection on the past today. In fact, long periods of time pass without the intrusion of a memory or a trigger. And I don't struggle with bitterness. After three decades of abuse, though, there will always be reflection. As I said earlier in the book, it's not my goal to forget. Remembering makes me thankful for my deliverance. Remembering reminds me of the lessons I've learned. Remembering magnifies the joy of today's blessings. And, most importantly, remembering increases my compassion for other victims. So I don't know why I would *ever* want to forget being abused.

I have a heart for victims of all forms of abuse because I know how it feels to be abused. I also have a considerable number of close friends who were victims of sexual abuse. I feel compelled to be an advocate for them. Many well-intentioned people have no idea the additional pain they inflict by urging victims to simply let it go, get over it, forgive, and *forget*. And many times this advice comes from someone trying to offer spiritual advice. Instead, they inflict additional guilt and shame on victims because it is completely unrealistic to suggest a victim will ever be able to forget their abuse. They may forgive. They may move forward with their lives. They may learn to rise above their pain. And in time their wounds can heal, fading into a faint scar. But they will not forget, and no one should suggest they ought to. The desire of others to make the abuse fade into thin air not only diminishes the impact of the abuse, it diminishes the worth of the victim. It sends the message that the abuse itself is somehow less injurious than the discomfort inflicted by talking about it. Victims need to talk through their suffering and when someone tries to silence them, it inflicts guilt and shame. It also makes victims feel responsible for the repercussions of the abuse. So not only do they carry the wounds of being abused, they carry the weight of how their abuse affects everyone around them. I've watched this play out in the lives of people I know and love. And it is never easy to witness. It frustrates me.

The pressure to let it go makes the victim feel like he or she is supposed to just pretend like it didn't happen. Sometimes the abuser tries to convince the victim that they have exaggerated the abuse. That was the pressure I experienced. Dennis tried to suppress the truth by telling me I was overreacting or by convincing me that my memory was faulty. But in other cases, even well-meaning family members are so uncomfortable with the subject of abuse that for their comfort they want the victim to act like it didn't happen. They are in denial. This denial can be especially strong in the extended family members of the abuser's family because they don't want to suffer embarrassment. I know of victims who have concealed their abuse for thirty-plus years because of the fear they would be vilified and hated by the family of their abuser for telling. They were more afraid of the loss of affection than the same abuse happening to additional victims as a result of keeping the secret.

In many families, there is spoken and unspoken pressure to keep family secrets. It's not permissible to share anything that reflects poorly on the family's reputation or image. But God made sure readers of the Bible did not overlook the humanity and sinfulness in the genealogy of Christ. At a time in history when women were not normally even mentioned in genealogies, we are reminded that Jesus' ancestry included Rahab the harlot and David's adultery with Bathsheba. There are many examples in the Bible of broken people facing their brokenness. The Bible is not a book of warm and fuzzy feel-good stories that denies life's harsh realities. We read many accounts of abuse in the pages of Scripture. Have you ever wondered why?

Why does God's Word reveal to us the many sins human beings have perpetrated on one another if He wants us to live in denial of our brokenness? He wants us to acknowledge and face our brokenness in order to heal and become whole. God never asks us to live in denial of truth. If our families or our churches ask that of us, it's important to remember they are not speaking for Him.

൞

In the first chapter of this book, I shared details of a falling-out between my father and me. I didn't revisit those details because I wanted to hurt or embarrass my dad. I included that part of the story because it is an important piece of the puzzle. The rejection I suffered from my dad was one of the reasons I concealed the abuse. I didn't feel emotionally safe with him. Turning to him for help or support was not an option for me. I was afraid. And what I feared was judgment. I had no fear of my dad holding me against a wall and clenching his fist in a physically threatening way as Dennis did. Instead I felt shame, knowing my dad was already disappointed in me. I so wanted my parents to be proud of me, but I felt the pain of having let them down. I was embarrassed to tell them my marriage was scary and falling apart badly in the first week. I wanted to hide from the truth. Maybe it was pride. But I couldn't imagine, in that moment, running to my dad's arms for comfort or help. Instead, that day I began a pattern of enabling Dennis' abuse and blaming myself that would last the next twenty-seven years. By concealing my abuse, I was telling Dennis that he had my permission and cooperation to abuse me again. But I thought I was protecting myself from embarrassment and shame. I was just a kid, and I was already taking on the role of an enabling battered wife.

Might I have made a different choice following that first incident if I'd felt cherished by my dad and confident he would offer comfort and protection rather than judgment? I think so. My guess is that many kids do not turn to their parents—when they ought to—out of fear of judgment and disapproval.

I do not *blame* my parents for my choices or even for letting me get married so young. And I don't carry the pain of my dad's rejection today. Our relationship is completely healed from *all* past wounds. We certainly haven't had the easiest father/daughter relationship. We have both hurt each other. However, what matters most is that those wounds are forgiven, they are healed, and we now enjoy a warm, loving relationship.

I love my dad. I know he loves me. And in the last year or so, I finally have felt the love and acceptance from him that I used to long for, which is why it's especially hard for me to include the hurtful words he has spoken to me in the past. But if sharing the details might influence even one single father to be more intentional in nurturing his daughter's self-worth, I think my dad would agree that the details should be shared. Sharing our past sin is a part of facing our brokenness, and none of us is alone in being broken.

Many parts of this book were painful for me to write and relive. I allowed myself to be treated with such contempt for so many years. I shake my head remembering how I once pursued, pleaded with, and apologized to an abusive bully. In hindsight, I am dismayed at the way I begged him not to be mad at me in response to his abuse. I blamed myself. I groveled. I cried. I was a doormat. Some of you will never be able understand why I allowed myself to be berated and mistreated for so long. But those of you who have walked a similar path understand completely. And I am not ashamed to identify with you.

I'm not proud to put in print the language I used the night on the front porch when Dennis threatened to blow his brains out. I wish I had not been guilty of infidelity in 1981. That chapter was hard to write. But it's all a part of my story. God doesn't want me to feel shame. I've repented. I'm forgiven. I have no reason to hide my brokenness from anyone. That I could possibly help another young woman to avoid some of the pitfalls of abuse that trapped me for years is way more important than my not being embarrassed. It is my strongest motivation for writing this book. I know from experience how isolating abuse is. Victims feel alone. Even our closest family members—who know we have been abused—often cannot relate to us or fully understand the effects of abuse that plague us for years after the abuse stops. It is comforting, reassuring, and validating to know there are other people who get it, who comprehend the depth of the wounds. Every book I have ever read on the topic of abuse or narcissistic personality disorder has helped me not only to understand the dynamic of abuse, but to know I am not alone.

As a victim, I did not understand why I was being treated the way Dennis treated me. I spent so much of my life trying to figure out how I could avoid the abuse by changing myself and my behavior. It was so affirming and comforting to hear my counselor say, "Shari, Dennis would have treated any wife the way he treated you. You could not have been a good enough wife to be treated differently. The abuse is about who he is, not who you are." You would think I could have figured that out on my own. But I needed to hear those words. It relieved me of the false guilt I carried for never being "good enough." I felt that way before I ever met Dennis. And I know there's a connection between the way I viewed myself and my willingness to accept being treated so badly for so long.

I'm thankful I have learned the value of boundaries and self-respect in the last ten years. And I'm thankful I have realized that it isn't the end of the world if someone disapproves of me. In *Bird by Bird: Some Instructions on Writing and Life*, Anne Lamott says this:

> Remember that you own what happened to you. If your childhood was less than ideal, you may have been raised thinking that if you told the truth about what really went on in your family, a long bony white finger would emerge from a cloud and point to you, while a chilling voice thundered, 'We *told* you not to tell.' But that was then. Just put down on paper everything you can remember . . . and we will deal with libel later on.

I certainly have not shared everything I remember. But there is no detail of my life I would be unwilling to reflect on and share if I believed it could help someone else. Living in the past is not good. But reflecting on the past, even a painful past, is positive and necessary for healing. Don't let anyone convince you otherwise. I am inspired and empowered to forge ahead as I reflect on how much I have already overcome.

Epilogue

"If we are honest and genuine, we are not afraid to show our wounds. 'To be alive is to be broken,' states Brennan Manning in The Ragamuffin Gospel... We can say, 'Here, look! This should have killed me – this battle wound right here, and here and here. These are my scars. Take a good look at where I am imperfect and even downright disgusting. It is an amazing thing that I live, but I do! You can be just as amazed as I am at the goodness of God. Because Jesus lives and has set me free, so I live and am free. The very pain that ought to have destroyed me has actually made me stronger and more alive." – Kim V. Engelmann

In *The Gift of Fear*, Gavin De Becker makes this strong statement: "The first time a woman is hit, she is a victim and the second time, she is a volunteer." Some people would argue that it's not that simple. I contend that it isn't that simple. I think remaining a victim is tied to what we believe—about God as well as ourselves.

It was only when I started to believe I really did have a choice that I was able to act on my own behalf and refuse to continue being abused. During my twenty-seven years as a victim, I spent a lot of time analyzing the reasons my abuser behaved the way he did. I tried to understand the deep insecurities that he was trying to overcompensate for with his bullying behavior. I knew he was a needy person, and I wanted to help him. But I did not have the power to change Dennis or to make him want to change. I finally accepted that and took responsibility for me. "Every human behavior can be explained by what precedes it, but that does not excuse it, and we must hold abusive men accountable," De Becker writes. Because of four years spent in counseling, I made the discovery that I did indeed have choices. I did not have to remain a victim. But I had to understand my role in the abuse and change myself.

The hardest realization for me to face was that I had literally been conditioning Dennis to treat me badly by pursuing (with apologies, pleading, buffering, and smoothing things over) in response to his abuse. Please don't misunderstand. I am not saying I caused him to abuse me. But my response was unhealthy and codependent. Whenever I did these things, I was simply trying to survive a hostile environment. I didn't mind being the one to apologize if it put an end to tension or strife. I couldn't see that I was giving my abuser exactly what he craved: power. He alone got to decide when a fight would be over. He would indulge in long periods of silence as a way to punish me, but I was not capable of enforcing consequences for bad behavior or boundary violations. I didn't even require an *apology*. All he had to do was crack a joke and make me laugh. That was my signal that things were okay again. I just wanted the fighting to be over at any cost. And my willingness to be continually exploited made him feel powerful.

An explosion of rage brought despair. A light moment brought relief. A good day offered hope. I strongly identified with De Becker's description of the way an abuser keeps hope alive in his victim. "He gives punishment and reward unpredictably, so that any day now, any moment now, he'll be his great old self, his honeymoon self, and this provides an ingredient that is essential to keeping the woman from leaving: hope." Being an eternal optimist when it comes to relationships and reconciliation, I consistently focused on the potential for change. And that served my abuser well. It took a long time to come to the realization that the only hope I had was false hope.

Looking back, I am thankful I was able finally to give up that false hope. Real hope inspires and empowers. False hope deflates and paralyzes. The false hope of the honeymoon cycle is just a spoke in the wheel of domestic abuse. I did not learn that until after my divorce. But as I studied family relations, psychology, and interpersonal communication in my college courses, I knew I had finally broken the cycle by saying first to myself and then to Dennis "I've had enough." But that alone wasn't enough. I had to back those words up with actions. You have to do more than stand up; you have to stand your ground.

One of the things that helped me immensely in my being able to give up my false hope was my counseling sessions with Floyd. I cannot stress enough how critical a role professional counseling played in what I would define as my self-discovery process. Going back to school was important. It gave me a sense of independence and confidence that I had lacked my entire adult life. I proved to myself that I could do things I never believed I could do. I dared to believe I could make it on my own. But it was the counseling that made me look deep within myself and see my behaviors differently. I'm thankful I was able to meet that challenge head on.

Self-sacrificing, noble, strong, resilient, and long-suffering became my identity in my marriage to Dennis. Those were all attributes I could feel good about. But counseling exposed to me that I was constantly self-protecting (not self-sacrificing). Rather than loving Dennis enough to stand up to him and challenge his behavior (for his betterment), far too often I gave in to him to avoid the consequences of his wrath. I appeased. I walked on eggshells. I excused his behavior in order to let him off the hook. I praised, always trying to bolster his ego. (I did not know the term "narcissistic supply" back then, but I knew how to provide it.) I did all of this for my own survival and comfort. My role was hard to face. But once my eyes were opened, remaining in that enabling role was not an option for me. As I said in my first book: "Once I had seen the ways in which my own unhealthy behavior had been an essential element in the toxicity, I simply could not remain in that role knowingly."

If I am proud of myself for anything I have accomplished, I guess one of the biggest things would be facing my own toxicity and flaws with humility and the desire to change. None of us will ever change in any way without first having the desire and the willingness to confront ourselves honestly. But it's important to remind ourselves that we can only change the present and the future. None of us can change the mistakes of the past. Once we've acknowledged those mistakes and asked forgiveness, we have to stop beating ourselves up. This is the area where I have experienced the most personal growth over the past year. When I began writing this book, I was still beating myself up and feeling guilty—as a mother in particular. Today I am not.

One of the most important reasons for getting out of an abusive relationship *is* for the sake of your children, though. Don't think you're doing them any favors by sticking around. One day they will tell you how wrong you were. And your children may even struggle to have the proper respect for you because they have picked up on cues from your abusive spouse. It's not uncommon for adult children to take on the abusive parent's condescending attitude toward the parent who willingly accommodates disrespect and tolerates abusive behavior over a long period of time.

I wouldn't have been a perfect parent under any circumstances. I am quite aware of my inadequacies. But I believe I might have been a different parent in a different marriage. Marry a person who will bring out the best in you, not the worst. This is especially important when it comes to raising children.

Since none of us can change the mistakes of the past, we must remind ourselves to focus on the beautiful redemption that is found in Christ. God works all things for the good of those who love Him (Romans 8:28). His restoration isn't typically instantaneous. It is often a process. Even still, while undergoing the process of being transformed, there is grace. I am learning to extend grace to myself along with others. God loves me. He is interested in me. And if He would give His Son for my redemption, there is nothing I need that He will not provide. If He allows me to go through suffering, it is for my ultimate good. I believe that with all my heart. I believe it for myself, and I believe it for those I love.

I have seen God's grace and redemption at work in my life in such obvious and profound ways. The last ten years have brought many blessings and the greatest joys I have ever known. There would surely not be a testimony of deliverance without the battle, but I have gotten away from viewing everything as a test of my performance. God knows my limitations better than I do. He knows I need His strength to pass any test put in my path. It's my faith that needs to be strengthened through trials. The battle is His, not mine.

My current pastor, Troy Rackliffe, recently spoke on David and reminded us that it was David's confidence in *God's power* to slay Goliath that enabled him to take the battlefield courageously and defeat Goliath. David wasn't relying on *his* armor, *his* strength, *his* skill, or the time *he'd* spent proving himself with a sling. David believed that *God* would deliver him based on all the previous times God had delivered him. God had proven His faithfulness to David through each instance of deliverance. And God has proven His faithfulness to me. That does not mean that my will and God's will are always in perfect alignment, but in every struggle I am confident He is working all things for my good.

God has a plan. No matter what happens to us, there is an opportunity to glorify Him. He gets glory from my suffering as I use what I have learned to reach out and help others. That in turn is a gift to me. It gives meaning and value to all my trials and tribulations. And I can think of no greater reward in this life than knowing I have lessened someone else's pain and isolation through sharing my own.

I do not regret the pain in my life. Suffering has increased my capacity for empathy and understanding. It has made me a better and more compassionate friend. And it has magnified the joy in my life. You don't realize it until you are delivered, but suffering can be a gift.

Most people talk about a happy life. But really, the best life is a satisfied life. People who recognize that their grief matured them, bettered them, tempered them, and humbled them, may still carry the burning jewel that sometimes stings, and yet they are satisfied. Their life is meaningful and important to them, and they want to play it out to the end. Such a person has a better quality of life than those who have never suffered and are content to paddle in shallow waters all their days.
— *Jeri Massi*

Suggested Reading

A Place of Healing: Wrestling with the Mysteries of Suffering, Pain and God's Sovereignty by Joni Eareckson Tada (Colorado Spring: David C. Cook, 2010)

Boundaries: When to Say Yes, How to Say No to Take Control of Your Life by Henry Cloud and John Townsend (Grand Rapids: Zondervan, 2002)

Boundaries in Marriage By Henry Cloud and John Townsend (Zondervan; 2002)

Mending the Soul: Understanding and Healing Abuse by Steven R. Tracy (Zondervan; 2008)

Running in Circles: How False Spirituality Traps Us in Unhealthy Relationships by Kim V. Engelmann (Chicago: IVP Books, 2007)

The Emotionally Destructive Relationship by Leslie Vernick (Eugene: Harvest House Publishers, 2007)

The Gift of Fear: And Other Survival Signals that Protect us from Violence by Gavin De Becker (New York: Dell, 1999)

Trusting God: Even When Life Hurts! by Jerry Bridges and Eugene H. Peterson (Colorado Springs: NavPress, 2008)

When People are Big and God is Small: Overcoming Peer Pressure, Codependency, and the Fear of Man by Edward T. Welch (Philipsburg: P & R Publishing, 1997)

Why Does He Do That? Inside the Minds of Angry and Controlling Men by Lundy Bancroft (New York: Berkley Publishing Group, 2002)

Why is it Always About You? The Seven Deadly Sins of Narcissism by Sandy Hotchkiss (New York: Free Press, 2002)

www.ingramcontent.com/pod-product-compliance
Lightning Source LLC
Chambersburg PA
CBHW031441040426
42444CB00007B/914